This Belongs to:
        Christopher McAuley

(C)Disney

A BOOK OF MYTHS

A Book of MYTHS

Selected and retold by
ROGER LANCELYN GREEN

Illustrated by
JOAN KIDDELL-MONROE

LONDON: J. M. DENT & SONS LTD
NEW YORK: E. P. DUTTON & CO. INC.

ROGER LANCELYN GREEN *was born on 2nd November 1918 at Norwich, but has spent most of his life at Poulton-Lancelyn in Cheshire, where his ancestors have been Lords of the Manor for thirty generations. He spent most of his childhood at home, owing to ill health, but in 1937 entered Merton College, Oxford, where he took an honours degree in English Language and Literature, followed by the post-graduate degree of Bachelor of Letters, and later was Deputy Librarian of the college for five years. He has also been a professional actor, an antiquarian bookseller, a schoolmaster and a Research Fellow at Liverpool University for short periods. Since 1950 he has lived at Poulton-Lancelyn and devoted most of his time to writing.*

Besides scholarly works on Andrew Lang, Lewis Carroll, A. E. W. Mason, J. M. Barrie and others, he has written many books for young readers. These include adventure stories such as 'The Theft of the Golden Cat' (1955), fairy-tale fantasies such as 'The Land of the Lord High Tiger' (1958), and romances set in Greece of the legendary period such as 'Mystery at Mycenae' (1957), and 'The Luck of Troy' (1961). But he is best known for his retelling of the old myths and legends, from 'King Arthur' (1953) and 'Robin Hood' (1956) to 'Heroes of Greece and Troy' (1960) and 'Myths of the Norsemen' (1962). He has visited Egypt once and Greece many times, and has written about them for young readers, telling of their history as well as of their legends —his own favourites being 'Old Greek Fairy Tales' (1958), his adventure story set in ancient Greece, Scandinavia and Britain, 'The Land Beyond the North' (1958), 'Ancient Egypt' (1963), and 'A Book of Myths'.

ISBN: 0 460 05066 4

A BOOK OF MYTHS
is
Dedicated
to
ITS FIRST READER
ENID GRIFFITHS
AND TO HER FAMILY

'Dust of the stars was under our feet, glitter of stars above—
Wrecks of our wrath dropped reeling down as we fought and
  we spurned and we strove.
Worlds upon worlds we tossed aside, and scattered them to and
  fro,
Hewing our way to Valhalla, a million years ago!'

Rudyard Kipling.

CONTENTS

PROLOGUE

How the Myths were Made

THE STORIES in this book are some of the oldest in the world. But they were told and retold, altered and reshaped so often, even before they were written down, that we can neither say when they began nor what they were like at first.

Probably the earliest myths were told as soon as the earliest men and women began to think—though we do not even know if they began to think suddenly, in this way, or gradually over many thousands of years.

In a moment—or in a millennium—they ceased to be animals and became human beings, and, as a very small child does, they started to ask questions. Why does the sun rise and set every day? How did we first learn to make and use a fire? How did the world begin? What happens when we die? Why do the crops and trees produce grain and fruit each year?—and is there anything we can do to make sure they grow next year?

All over the world the same main answer was found: 'In the beginning God created the heaven and the earth.' When Man ceased to be an animal he was given the knowledge that Something or Someone greater than himself had made him and all the world, was in some sense his Father, and in some way could give him another sort of life after earthly death.

What went wrong after that cannot be discussed here. In some way 'Adam' and 'Eve' ate of the forbidden fruit, and were left to fend for themselves, and make up their own stories and guesses and half-truths about the beginnings and the working of the world. Somewhere in the back of their minds was a vague memory or knowledge of the truth, but stories and inventions of all sorts got piled up in front of it for thousands of years, and gods and devils and monsters without number were invented. Then one tribe conquered another, or one civilization another, and the ideas of the conquerors were forced upon the conquered, and from this grew stories of the battles between the old gods and the new.

Often the different ideas of God were joined together as a number of tribes became a single nation or people; but usually in this process each section kept its own god, and presently these gods became a family, generally with the god of the most powerful tribe as their overlord, or even their father.

This is probably what happened in ancient Greece. The first Greeks came in from the north about 2000 B.C. and conquered whoever lived there already. And the Greek gods conquered the gods of the previous inhabitants, and so the stories of the war of Zeus and the Olympians against Cronos and the Titans came into existence and a myth was made.

But the Greeks who settled in different parts of the country had different gods at the beginning, and began to wonder about the differences only when the various states grew into some kind of nation with a High King, such as Agamemnon of Mycenae, to command them all in time of war. They were all kings of separate little states—Achilles and Ajax and Odysseus and the rest—but Agamemnon was a little higher; and when he summoned them they all obeyed and set out for the siege of Troy under his command.

In just the same way, Athena was the goddess of Athens and Apollo was the god of Delphi, Hera of Argos and Demeter of Eleusis; but Zeus was the king of the gods, just as Agamemnon was of the lesser kings on earth, and came at his command to fight the Titans or the Giants. Sometimes they rebelled, as an earthly king might—and Zeus took proper steps, throwing Hephaestus out of Heaven or hanging Hera from the sky with weights attached to her feet, and so on.

Then about 1000 B.C. came a fresh wave of Greek invaders from the north, and the country was overrun once more. But this time no new gods came to cast the old ones out of Heaven—though the myths say that Zeus expected that they would, and was only saved by the good Titan Prometheus, a survivor from the gods whom Zeus had overcome, who told him how to prevent the same thing from happening again.

The old stories about the gods were treasured, however. A certain amount was forgotten as to their meaning; and legends of real happenings, such as the siege of Troy, were added to them as well as a few complete fairy tales; and then the poets from Homer onwards began to weave them into epics and plays.

As the Greeks grew more and more civilized, the wisest and most thoughtful of them began to realize that most of the stories told about the gods had grown up in some way or other around and in front of the true story about God—as we find in the works of a great poet like Aeschylus, or in the teachings of Socrates.

The stories which were left behind as part of religion, but treasured and retold as part of literature, are the myths of which some of the most famous are included in this book.

They are a strange mixture of the cruel and horrific with the beautiful and the mysterious. In the same story you will find the ideas of the frightened savage in the jungle as the lightning flashes and the thunderbolt splits the oak tree under which he is sheltering, and the poetic fancy that is the unseen truth put into a visible form. To find stories like that of Cronos swallowing his children we have to go to the most primitive savages of central Australia a hundred years ago. But when the wonder and loveliness of the hills and valleys and streams and the dark blue sea of Greece call up fancies of nymphs and fairies, of Apollo with his lyre and the Muses singing on Mount Helicon, we may not exactly believe in them, but we understand them, and feel that they stood for something real.

Man, in his struggle against cold and hunger, or overpowering heat and drought, invented evil beings who were the things themselves, or their causes, in just the same way as he made the good things and instincts of life into real beings about whom stories and myths were made. The sun grew dim and the terrible cold of the arctic regions came over the earth—and the Scandinavians told how Loki had killed Baldur the Sun-god. The flowers and corn grew suddenly out of the barren earth and the wonderful spring of Greece was spread over the hills and valleys—and the Greeks told how Persephone came up out of the realm of Hades to comfort her sorrowing mother Demeter.

The stories in this book are taken from the myths of those countries which became sufficiently civilized, while still believing in them to a greater or lesser extent, to collect and arrange them and tell them in magnificent poems and plays, stories and sagas.

But behind them you will catch from time to time a glimpse of the early savage world, and of the strange conflict between a high religion and a collection of grotesque stories about even the chief god.

Thus, among the Bushmen of central Africa almost a hundred years ago, the hunter Qing was asked about Cagn, the god whom he worshipped: 'Is Cagn good or malicious? How do you pray to him?' And he answered, in a low imploring tone: 'O Cagn! O Cagn! are we not your children? Do you not see our hunger? Give us food!' And then, said Qing: 'He gives us both hands full.'

Yet the same Bushmen told tales of Cagn as a giant mantis or grasshopper who made the moon out of his shoe—and the moon is the colour of the dust in Bushman-land; how the mantis was defeated by a cat who happened to be singing a song about a lynx; how he was swallowed by the father of his adopted daughter, and then disgorged alive and well—and many other stories of the kind.

This whole background to mythology is summed up in the sonnet by Andrew Lang which is based on what Qing the Bushman had said:

'Once Cagn was like a father, kind and good,
    But he was spoiled by fighting many things;
He wars upon the lions in the wood,
    And breaks the thunder-bird's tremendous wings;
But still we cry to him—*We are thy brood*—
    Oh Cagn, be merciful!—and us he brings
To herds of elands, and great store of food,
    And in the desert opens water-springs.'

So Qing, King Nqsha's Bushman hunter, spoke,
    Beside the camp-fire, by the fountain fair,
When all were weary, and soft clouds of smoke
    Were fading, fragrant, in the twilit air;
And suddenly in each man's heart there woke
    A pang, a sacred memory of prayer.

EGYPTIAN

THE STORY OF RA

IN THE beginning, before there was any land of Egypt, all was darkness, and there was nothing but a great waste of water called Nu. The power of Nu was such that there arose out of the darkness a great shining egg, and this was Ra.

Now Ra was all-powerful, and he could take many forms. His power and the secret of it lay in his hidden name; but if he spoke other names, that which he named came into being.

'I am Khepera at the dawn, and Ra at noon, and Tum in the evening,' he said. And the sun rose and passed across the sky and set for the first time.

Then he named Shu, and the first winds blew; he named Refnut the spitter, and the first rain fell. Next he named Geb, and the earth came into being; he named the goddess Nut, and she was the sky arched over the earth with her feet on one horizon and her hands on the other; he named Hapi, and the great River Nile flowed through Egypt and made it fruitful.

After this Ra named all things that are upon the earth, and they grew. Last of all he named mankind, and there were men and women in the land of Egypt.

Then Ra took on the shape of a man and became the first Pharaoh, ruling over the whole country for thousands and

thousands of years, and giving such harvests that for ever afterwards the Egyptians spoke of the good things 'which happened
in the time of Ra'.

But, being in the form of a man, Ra grew old. In time men no
longer feared him or obeyed his laws. They laughed at him,
saying: 'Look at Ra! His bones are like silver, his flesh like gold,
his hair is the colour of lapis lazuli!'

Ra was angry when he heard this, and he was more angry still
at the evil deeds which men were doing in disobedience to his
laws. So he called together the gods whom he had made—Shu
and Tefnut and Geb and Nut—and he also summoned Nu.
Soon the gods gathered about Ra in his Secret Place, and the
goddesses also. But mankind knew nothing of what was happening, and continued to jeer at Ra and to break his command-
ments. Then Ra spoke to Nu before the assembled gods: 'Eldest of
the gods, you who made me; and you gods whom I have made:
look upon mankind who came into being at a glance of my Eye.
See how men plot against me; hear what they say of me; tell me
what I should do to them. For I will not destroy mankind until I
have heard what you advise.'

Then Nu said: 'My son Ra, the god greater than he who made
him and mightier than those whom he has created, turn your
mighty Eye upon them and send destruction upon them in the
form of your daughter the goddess Sekhmet.'

Ra answered: 'Even now fear is falling upon them and they are
fleeing into the deserts and hiding themselves in the mountains in
terror at the sound of my voice.'

'Send against them the glance of your Eye in the form of
Sekhmet!' cried all the other gods and goddesses, bowing before
Ra until their foreheads touched the ground.

So at the terrible glance from the Eye of Ra his daughter
Sekhmet came into being, the fiercest of all goddesses. Like a lion
she rushed upon her prey, and her chief delight was in slaughter
and her pleasure was in blood. At the bidding of Ra she came into
Upper and Lower Egypt to slay those who had scorned and
disobeyed him: she killed them among the mountains which lie

on either side of the Nile, and down beside the river, and in the burning deserts. All whom she saw she slew, rejoicing in slaughter and the taste of blood.

Presently Ra looked out over the land and saw what Sekhmet had done. Then he called to her, saying: 'Come, my daughter, and tell me how you have obeyed my commands.'

Sekhmet answered with the terrible voice of a lioness as she tears her prey: 'By the life which you have given me, I have indeed done vengeance on mankind, and my heart rejoices.'

Now for many nights the Nile ran red with blood, and Sekhmet's feet were red as she went hither and thither through all the land of Egypt slaying and slaying.

Presently Ra looked out over the earth once more, and now his heart was stirred with pity for men, even though they had rebelled against him. But none could stop the cruel goddess Sekhmet, not even Ra himself: she must cease from slaying of her own accord —and Ra saw that this could only come about through cunning.

So he gave his command: 'Bring before me swift messengers who will run upon the earth as silently as shadows and with the speed of the storm winds.' When these were brought he said to them: 'Go as fast as you can up the Nile to where it flows fiercely over the rocks and among the islands of the First Cataract; go to the isle that is called Elephantinē and bring from it a great store of the red ochre which is to be found there.'

The messengers sped on their way and returned with the blood-red ochre to Heliopolis, the city of Ra where stand the stone obelisks with points of gold that are like fingers pointing to the sun. It was night when they came to the city, but all day the women of Heliopolis had been brewing beer as Ra bade them.

Ra came to where the beer stood waiting in seven thousand jars, and the gods came with him to see how by his wisdom he would save mankind.

'Mingle the red ochre of Elephantinē with the barley-beer,' said Ra, and it was done, so that the beer gleamed red in the moonlight like the blood of men.

'Now take it to the place where Sekhmet proposes to slay men

B

when the sun rises,' said Ra. And while it was still night the seven thousand jars of beer were taken and poured out over the fields so that the ground was covered to the depth of nine inches—three times the measure of the palm of a man's hand—with the strong beer, whose other name is 'sleep-maker'.

When day came Sekhmet the terrible came also, licking her lips at the thought of the men whom she would slay. She found the place flooded and no living creature in sight; but she saw the beer which was the colour of blood, and she thought it was blood indeed—the blood of those whom she had slain.

Then she laughed with joy, and her laughter was like the roar of a lioness hungry for the kill. Thinking that it was indeed blood, she stooped and drank. Again and yet again she drank, laughing with delight; and the strength of the beer mounted to her brain, so that she could no longer slay.

At last she came reeling back to where Ra was waiting; and that day she had not killed even a single man.

Then Ra said: 'You come in peace, sweet one.' And her name was changed to Hathor, and her nature was changed also to the sweetness of love and the strength of desire. And henceforth Hathor laid low men and women only with the great power of love. But for ever after her priestesses drank in her honour of the beer of Heliopolis coloured with the red ochre of Elephantinē when they celebrated her festival each New Year.

So mankind was saved, and Ra continued to rule, old though he was. But the time was drawing near when he must leave the earth to reign for ever in the heavens, letting the younger gods rule in his place. For dwelling in the form of a man, of a Pharaoh of Egypt, Ra was losing his wisdom; yet he continued to reign, and no one could take his power from him, since that power dwelt in his secret name which none knew but himself. If only anyone could discover his Name of Power, Ra would reign no longer on earth; but only by magic arts was this possible.

Geb and Nut had children: these were the younger gods whose day had come to rule, and their names were Osiris and Isis, Nephthys and Set. Of these Isis was the wisest: she was cleverer

than a million men, her knowledge was greater than that of a million of the noble dead. She knew all things in heaven and earth, except only for the Secret Name of Ra, and that she now set herself to learn by guile.

Now Ra was growing older every day. As he passed across the land of Egypt his head shook from side to side with age, his jaw trembled, and he dribbled at the mouth as do the very old among men. As his spittle fell upon the ground it made mud, and this Isis took in her hands and kneaded together as if it had been dough. Then she formed it into the shape of a serpent, making the first cobra—the *uraeus*, which ever after was the symbol of royalty worn by Pharaoh and his queen.

Isis placed the first cobra in the dust of the road by which Ra passed each day as he went through his two kingdoms of Upper and Lower Egypt. As Ra passed by the cobra bit him and then vanished into the grass. But the venom of its bite coursed through his veins, and for a while Ra was speechless, save for one great cry of pain which rang across the earth from the eastern to the western horizon. The gods who followed him crowded round, asking: 'What is it? What ails you?' But he could find no words; his lips trembled and he shuddered in all his limbs, while the poison spread over his body as the Nile spreads over Egypt at the inundation. When at last he could speak, Ra said: 'Help me, you whom I have made. Something has hurt me, and I do not know what it is. I created all things, yet this thing I did not make. It is a pain such as I have never known before, and no other pain is equal to it. Yet who can hurt me?—for none knows my Secret Name which is hidden in my heart, giving me all power and guarding me against

the magic of both wizard and witch. Nevertheless as I passed
through the world which I have created, through the two lands
that are my special care, something stung me. It is like fire, yet it is
not fire; it is like water and not water. I burn and I shiver, while
all my limbs tremble. So call before me all the gods who have skill
in healing and knowledge of magic, and wisdom that reaches to
the heavens.'

Then all the gods came to Ra, weeping and lamenting at the
terrible thing which had befallen him. With them came Isis the
healer, the queen of magic, who breathes the breath of life and
knows words to revive those who are dying. And she said:

'What is it, divine father? Has a snake bitten you? Has a
creature of your own creating lifted up its head against you? I will
drive it out by the magic that is mine, and make it tremble and fall
down before your glory.'

'I went by the usual way through my two lands of Egypt,'
answered Ra, 'for I wished to look upon all that I had made. And
as I went I was bitten by a snake which I did not see—a snake that
I had not created. Now I burn as if with fire and shiver as if my
veins were filled with water, and the sweat runs down my face as
it runs down the faces of men on the hottest days of summer.'

'Tell me your Secret Name,' said Isis in a sweet, soothing
voice. 'Tell it me, divine father; for only by speaking your name
in my spells can I cure you.'

Then Ra spoke the many names that were his: 'I am Maker of
Heaven and Earth,' he said. 'I am Builder of the Mountains. I am
Source of the Waters throughout all the world. I am Light and
Darkness. I am Creator of the Great River of Egypt. I am the
Kindler of the Fire that burns in the sky; yes, I am Khepera in the
morning, Ra at the noontide, and Tum in the evening.'

But Isis said never a word, and the poison had its way in the
veins of Ra. For she knew that he had told her only the names
which all men knew, and that his Secret Name, the Name of
Power, still lay hidden in his heart.

At last she said:

'You know well that the name which I need to learn is not

among those which you have spoken. Come, tell me the Secret Name, for if you do the poison will come forth and you will have an end of pain.'

The poison burned with a great burning, more powerful than any flame of fire, and Ra cried out at last:

'Let the Name of Power pass from my heart into the heart of Isis! But before it does, swear to me that you will tell it to no other save only the son whom you will have, whose name shall be Horus. And bind him first with such an oath that the name will remain with him and be passed on to no other gods or men.'

Isis the great magician swore the oath, and the knowledge of the Name of Power passed from the heart of Ra into hers.

Then she said: 'By the name which I know, let the poison go from Ra for ever!'

So it passed from him and he had peace. But he reigned upon earth no longer. Instead he took his place in the high heavens, travelling each day across the sky in the likeness of the sun itself, and by night crossing the underworld of Amenti in the Boat of Ra and passing through the twelve divisions of Duat where many dangers lurk. Yet Ra passes safely, and with him he takes those souls of the dead who know all the charms and prayers and words that must be said. And so that a man might not go unprepared for his voyage in the Boat of Ra, the Egyptians painted all the scenes of that journey on the walls of the tombs of the Pharaohs, with all the knowledge that was written in *The Book of the Dead*, of which a copy was buried in the grave of lesser men so that they too might read and come safely to the land beyond the west where the dead dwell.

ISIS AND OSIRIS

IN THE days before Ra had left the earth, before he had begun
to grow old, his great wisdom told him that if the goddess Nut
bore children, one of them would end his reign among men. So
Ra laid a curse upon Nut—that she should not be able to bear any
child upon any day in the year.

Full of sorrow, Nut went for help to Thoth, the thrice-great
god of wisdom and magic and learning, Ra's son, who loved her.
Thoth knew that the curse of Ra, once spoken, could never be
recalled, but in his wisdom he found a way of escape. He went to
Khonsu, the Moon-god, and challenged him to a contest at

14

draughts. Game after game they played and always Thoth won. The stakes grew higher and higher, but Khonsu wagered the most, for it was some of his own light that he risked and lost.

At last Khonsu would play no more. Then Thoth the thrice-great in wisdom gathered up the light which he had won and made it into five extra days which for ever after were set between the end of the old year and the beginning of the new. The year was of three hundred and sixty days before this, but the five days which were added, which were not days of any year, were ever afterwards held as days of festival in old Egypt.

But, since his match with Thoth, Khonsu the moon has not had enough light to shine throughout the month, but dwindles into darkness and then grows to his full glory again; for he had lost the light needed to make five whole days.

On the first of these days Osiris, the eldest son of Nut, was born, and the second day was set aside to be the birthday of Horus. On the third day the second son of Nut was born, dark Set, the lord of evil. On the fourth her daughter Isis first saw the light, and her second daughter Nephthys on the fifth. In this way the curse of Ra was both fulfilled and defeated: for the days on which the children of Nut were born belonged to no year.

When Osiris was born many signs and wonders were seen and heard throughout the world. Most notable was the voice which came from the holiest shrine in the temple at Thebes on the Nile, which today is called Karnak, speaking to a man called Pamyles bidding him proclaim to all men that Osiris, the good and mighty king, was born to bring joy to all the earth.

Pamyles did as he was bidden, and he also attended on the Divine Child and brought him up as a man among men.

When Osiris was grown up he married his sister Isis, a custom which the Pharaohs of Egypt followed ever after. And Set married Nephthys: for he too being a god could marry only a goddess.

After Isis by her craft had learned the Secret Name of Ra, Osiris became sole ruler of Egypt and reigned on earth as Ra had done. He found the people both savage and brutish, fighting among themselves and killing and eating one another. But Isis discovered the grain of both wheat and barley, which grew wild over the land with the other plants and was still unknown to man; and Osiris taught them how to plant the seeds when the Nile had risen in the yearly inundation and sunk again leaving fresh fertile mud over the fields; how to tend and water the crops; how to cut the corn when it was ripe, and how to thresh the grain on the threshing floors, dry it and grind it to flour and make it into bread. He showed them also how to plant vines and make the grapes into wine; and they knew already how to brew beer out of the barley.

When the people of Egypt had learned to make bread and eat only the flesh of such animals as he taught them were suitable, Osiris went on to teach them laws, and how to live peacefully and happily together, delighting themselves with music and poetry.

As soon as Egypt was filled with peace and plenty, Osiris set out over the world to bring his blessings upon other nations. While he was away he left Isis to rule over the land, which she did both wisely and well.

But Set the Evil One, their brother, envied Osiris and hated Isis. The more the people loved and praised Osiris, the more Set hated him; and the more good he did and the happier mankind became, the stronger grew Set's desire to kill his brother and rule in his place.

Isis, however, was so full of wisdom and so watchful that Set made no attempt to seize the throne while she was watching over the land of Egypt. And when Osiris returned from his travels Set was among the first to welcome him back and kneel in reverence before 'the good god Pharaoh Osiris'.

Yet he had made his plans, aided by seventy-two of his wicked friends and Aso the evil queen of Ethiopia. Secretly Set obtained the exact measurements of the body of Osiris, and caused a beautiful chest to be made that would fit only him. It was fashioned of the rarest and most costly woods: cedar brought from Lebanon, and ebony from Punt at the south end of the Red Sea— for no wood grows in Egypt except the soft and useless palm.

Then Set gave a great feast in honour of Osiris; but the other guests were the two-and-seventy conspirators. It was the greatest feast that had yet been seen in Egypt, and the foods were choicer, the wines stronger and the dancing girls more beautiful than ever before. When the heart of Osiris had been made glad with feasting and song, the chest was brought in, and all were amazed at its beauty.

Osiris marvelled at the rare cedar inlaid with ebony and ivory, with less rare gold and silver, and painted inside with figures of gods and birds and animals, and he desired it greatly.

'I will give this chest to whosoever fits it most exactly!' cried Set. And at once the conspirators began in turn to see if they could win it. But one was too tall and another too short; one was too fat and another too thin—and all tried in vain.

'Let me see if I will fit into this marvellous piece of work,' said Osiris, and he laid himself down in the chest while all gathered round breathlessly.

'I fit exactly, and the chest is mine!' cried Osiris.

'It is yours indeed, and shall be so for ever!' hissed Set as he banged down the lid. Then in desperate haste he and the conspirators nailed it shut and sealed every crack with molten lead, so that Osiris the man died in the chest and his spirit went west across the Nile into Duat the Place of Testing; but, beyond it to Amenti, where those live for ever who have lived well on earth and passed the judgments of Duat, he could not pass as yet.

Set and his companions took the chest which held the body of Osiris and cast it into the Nile; and Hapi the Nile-god carried it out into the Great Green Sea where it was tossed for many days until it came to the shore of Phoenicia near the city of Byblos. Here the waves cast it into a tamarisk tree that grew on the shore; and the tree shot out branches and grew leaves and flowers to make a fit resting-place for the body of the good god Osiris— and very soon that tree became famous throughout the land.

Presently King Malcander heard of it, and he and his wife, Queen Astarte, came to the seashore to gaze at the tree. By now the branches had grown together and hidden the chest which held the body of Osiris in the trunk itself. King Malcander gave orders that the tree should be cut down and fashioned into a great pillar for his palace. This was done, and all wondered at its beauty and fragrance: but none knew that it held the body of a god.

Meanwhile in Egypt Isis was in great fear. She had always known that Set was filled with evil and jealousy, but kindly Osiris would not believe in his brother's wickedness. But Isis knew as soon as her husband was dead, though no one told her, and fled into the marshes of the delta carrying the baby Horus with her. She found shelter on a little island where the goddess Buto lived, and entrusted the divine child to her. And as a further safeguard against Set, Isis loosed the island from its foundations, and let it float so that no one could tell where to find it.

Then she went to seek for the body of Osiris. For, until he was buried with all the needful rites and charms, even his spirit could go no farther to the west than Duat, the Testing-place; and it could not come to Amenti.

Back and forth over the land of Egypt wandered Isis, but never a trace could she find of the chest in which lay the body of Osiris. She asked all whom she met, but no one had seen it—and in this matter her magic powers could not help her.

At last she questioned the children who were playing by the riverside, and at once they told her that just such a chest as she described had floated past them on the swift stream and out into the Great Green Sea.

Then Isis wandered on the shore, and again and again it was the children who had seen the chest floating by and told her which way it had gone. And because of this, Isis blessed the children and decreed that ever afterwards children should speak words of wisdom and sometimes tell of things to come.

At length Isis came to Byblos and sat down by the seashore. Presently the maidens who attended on Queen Astarte came down to bathe at that place; and when they returned out of the water Isis taught them how to plait their hair—which had never been done before. When they went up to the palace a strange and wonderful perfume seemed to cling to them; and Queen Astarte marvelled at it, and at their plaited hair, and asked them how it came to be so.

The maidens told her of the wonderful woman who sat by the seashore, and Queen Astarte sent for Isis, and asked her to serve in the palace and tend her children, the little Prince Maneros and the baby Dictys, who was ailing sorely. For she did not know that the strange woman who was wandering alone at Byblos was the greatest of all the goddesses of Egypt.

Isis agreed to this, and very soon the baby Dictys was strong and well, though she did no more than give him her finger to suck. But presently she became fond of the child, and thought to make him immortal, which she did by burning away his mortal parts while she flew round and round him in the form of a swallow. Astarte, however, had been watching her secretly; and when she saw that her baby seemed to be on fire she rushed into the room with a loud cry, and so broke the magic.

Then Isis took on her own form, and Astarte crouched down in terror when she saw the shining goddess and learned who she was.

Malcander and Astarte offered her gifts of all the richest treasures in Byblos, but Isis asked only for the great tamarisk pillar which held up the roof, and for what it contained.

When it was given to her, she caused it to open and took out the chest of Set. But the pillar she gave back to Malcander and

Astarte; and it remained the most sacred object in Byblos, since it had once held the body of a god.

When the chest which had become the coffin of Osiris was given to her, Isis flung herself down on it with so terrible a cry of sorrow that little Dictys died at the very sound. But Isis at length caused the chest to be placed on a ship which King Malcander provided for her, and set out for Egypt. With her went Maneros, the young prince of Byblos: but he did not remain with her for long, since his curiosity proved his undoing. For as soon as the ship had left the land Isis retired to where the chest of Set lay, and opened the lid. Maneros crept up behind her and peeped over her shoulder: but Isis knew he was there and, turning, gave him one glance of anger—and he fell backwards over the side of the ship into the sea.

Next morning, as the ship was passing the Phaedrus River, its strong current threatened to carry them out of sight of land. But Isis grew angry and placed a curse on the river, so that its stream dried up from that day.

She came safely to Egypt after this, and hid the chest in the marshes of the delta while she hastened to the floating island where Buto was guarding Horus.

But it chanced that Set came hunting wild boars with his dogs, hunting by night after his custom, since he loved the darkness in which evil things abound. By the light of the moon he saw the chest of cedar wood inlaid with ebony and ivory, with gold and silver, and recognized it.

At the sight hatred and anger came upon him in a red cloud, and he raged like a panther of the south. He tore open the chest, took the body of Osiris, and rent it into fourteen pieces which, by his divine strength, he scattered up and down the whole length of the Nile so that the crocodiles might eat them.

'It is not possible to destroy the body of a god!' cried Set. 'Yet I have done it—for I have destroyed Osiris!' His laughter echoed through the land, and all who heard it trembled and hid.

Now Isis had to begin her search once more. This time she had helpers, for Nephthys left her wicked husband Set and came to join her sister. And Anubis, the son of Set and Nephthys, taking the form of a jackal, assisted in the search. When Isis travelled over the land she was accompanied and guarded by seven scorpions. But when she searched on the Nile and among the many

streams of the delta she made her way in a boat made of papyrus:
and the crocodiles, in their reverence for the goddess, touched
neither the rent pieces of Osiris nor Isis herself. Indeed ever afterwards anyone who sailed the Nile in a boat made of papyrus was
safe from them, for they thought that it was Isis still questing after
the pieces of her husband's body.

Slowly, piece by piece, Isis recovered the fragments of Osiris.
And wherever she did so, she formed by magic the likeness of his
whole body and caused the priests to build a shrine and perform
his funeral rites. And so there were thirteen places in Egypt which
claimed to be the burial place of Osiris. In this way also she made
it harder for Set to meddle further with the body of the dead god.

One piece only she did not recover, for it had been eaten by
certain impious fishes; and their kind were accursed ever afterwards, and no Egyptian would touch or eat them.

Isis, however, did not bury any of the pieces in the places where
the tombs and shrines of Osiris stood. She gathered the pieces
together, rejoined them by magic, and by magic made a likeness of
the missing member so that Osiris was complete. Then she caused
the body to be embalmed and hidden away in a place of which she
alone knew. And after this the spirit of Osiris passed into Amenti
to rule over the dead until the last great battle, when Horus should
slay Set and Osiris would return to earth once more.

But as Horus grew in this world the spirit of Osiris visited him
often and taught him all that a great warrior should know—one
who was to fight against Set both in the body and in the spirit.

One day Osiris said to the boy: 'Tell me, what is the noblest
thing that a man can do?'

And Horus answered: 'To avenge his father and mother for
the evil done to them.'

This pleased Osiris, and he asked further: 'And what animal is
most useful for the avenger to take with him as he goes out to
battle?'

'A horse,' answered Horus promptly.

'Surely a lion would be better still?' suggested Osiris.

'A lion would indeed be the best for a man who needed help,' replied Horus; 'but a horse is best for pursuing a flying foe and cutting him off from escape.'

When he heard this Osiris knew that the time had come for Horus to declare war on Set, and bade him gather together a great army and sail up the Nile to attack him in the deserts of the south.

Horus gathered his forces and prepared to begin the war. And Ra himself, the shining father of the gods, came to his aid in his own divine boat that sails across the heavens and through the dangers of the underworld.

Before they set sail Ra drew Horus aside so as to gaze into his blue eyes: for whoever looks into them, of gods or men, sees the future reflected there. But Set was watching; and he took upon himself the form of a black pig—black as the thunder-cloud, fierce to look at, with tusks to strike terror into the bravest heart.

Meanwhile Ra said to Horus: 'Let me gaze into your eyes, and see what is to come of this war.' He gazed into the eyes of Horus, and their colour was that of the Great Green Sea when the summer sky turns it to deepest blue.

While he gazed the black pig passed by and distracted his attention, so that he exclaimed: 'Look at that! Never have I seen so huge and fierce a pig.'

And Horus looked; and he did not know that it was Set, but thought it was a wild boar out of the thickets of the north, and he was not ready with a charm or a word of power to guard himself against the enemy.

Then Set aimed a blow of fire at the eyes of Horus; and Horus shouted with the pain and was in a great rage. He knew now that it was Set; but Set had gone on the instant and could not be trapped.

Ra caused Horus to be taken into a dark room, and it was long before his eyes could see again as clearly as before. When he was recovered Ra had returned to the sky; but Horus was filled with joy that he could see once more, and as he set out up the Nile at the head of his army, the country on either side shared his joy and blossomed into spring.

There were many battles in that war, but the last and greatest was at Edfu, where the great temple of Horus stands to this day in memory of it. The forces of Set and Horus drew near to one another among the islands and the rapids of the First Cataract of the Nile. Set, in the form of a red hippopotamus of gigantic size, sprang up on the island of Elephantinē and uttered a great curse against Horus and against Isis:

'Let there come a terrible raging tempest and a mighty flood against my enemies!' he cried, and his voice was like the thunder rolling across the heavens from the south to the north.

At once the storm broke over the boats of Horus and his army; the wind roared and the water was heaped into great waves. But Horus held on his way, his own boat gleaming through the darkness, its prow shining like a ray of the sun.

Opposite Edfu, Set turned and stood at bay, straddling the whole stream of the Nile, so huge a red hippopotamus was he. But Horus took upon himself the shape of a handsome young man, twelve feet in height. His hand held a harpoon thirty feet long with a blade six feet wide at its point of greatest width.

Set opened his mighty jaws to destroy Horus and his followers when the storm should wreck their boats. But Horus cast his harpoon, and it struck deep into the head of the red hippopotamus, deep into his brain. And that one blow slew Set the great wicked one, the enemy of Osiris and the gods—and the red hippopotamus sank dead beside the Nile at Edfu.

The storm passed away, the flood sank and the sky was clear and blue once more. Then the people of Edfu came out to welcome Horus the avenger and lead him in triumph to the shrine over which the great temple now stands. And they sang the song of praise which the priests chanted ever afterwards when the yearly festival of Horus was held at Edfu:

'Rejoice, you who dwell in Edfu! Horus the great god, the lord of the sky, has slain the enemy of his father! Eat the flesh of the vanquished, drink the blood of the red hippopotamus, burn his bones with fire! Let him be cut in pieces, and the scraps be given to the cats, and the offal to the reptiles!

'Glory to Horus of the mighty blow, the brave one, the slayer, the wielder of the Harpoon, the only son of Osiris, Horus of Edfu, Horus the avenger!'

But when Horus passed from earth and reigned no more as the Pharaoh of Egypt, he appeared before the assembly of the gods, and Set came also in the spirit, and contended in words for the rule of the world. But not even Thoth the wise could give judgment. And so it comes about that Horus and Set still contend for the souls of men and for the rule of the world.

There were no more battles on the Nile or in the land of Egypt; and Osiris rested quietly in his grave, which (since Set could no longer disturb it) Isis admitted was on the island of Philae, the most sacred place of all, in the Nile a few miles upstream from Elephantinē.

But the Egyptians believed that the Last Battle was still to come —and that Horus would defeat Set in this also. And when Set was destroyed for ever, Osiris would rise from the dead and return to earth, bringing with him all those who had been his own faithful followers. And for this reason the Egyptians embalmed their dead and set the bodies away beneath towering pyramids of stone and deep in the tomb chambers of western Thebes, so that the blessed souls returning from Amenti should find them ready to enter again, and in them to live for ever on earth under the good god Osiris, Isis his queen and their son Horus.

BABYLONIAN

MARDUK THE AVENGER

EFORE the making of the earth, the forming of the Land of the Two Rivers which was later called Babylon, there was a great waste of waters. Apsu was the god of the fresh water, and Tiamat the goddess of the salt water, and from these two were born the gods and spirits of the deep.

Anshar and Kishar—'Male' and 'Female'—were the first of the gods born to Tiamat and Apsu and, being male and female, they married and had children, the two Great Gods, Anu and Enlil. Anu was lord of the heavens, and he made Heaven as a dwelling-place for the gods of his own family, the Anunnaki.

In time Anu's son Ea became chief god of the Anunnaki. But he was not able to remain the lord of all, for his son Marduk proved to be greater still in strength and courage.

Now although the great powers Apsu and Tiamat were the ancestors of all the younger gods, they did not love them. Indeed the sounds of joy coming from the great feasts in the Hall of Heaven made Apsu so angry and filled his heart with such hatred that he decided to destroy all the younger gods.

So he called his counsellor Mummu, who had been formed out of the sound of the waters murmuring together in the morning of time, and said:

'Come, let us go to Tiamat!'

They came to Tiamat, and Apsu said: 'The ways of the younger gods, our children and their offspring, are loathsome to me. I cannot rest by night because of them, nor can I find any relief from the sound of their doings. So now I will destroy them, and we will once more be at peace as we were before the beginning of the world.'

'What?' grumbled Tiamat. 'Destroy the creatures we have made? Certainly their ways are troublesome; but does Mummu think this is the best thing to do?'

'Destroy them, father Apsu,' murmured Mummu. 'Massacre them for their mutinous ways. Then you will have peace both by day and night.'

When Apsu heard this his face grew radiant with delight, for he desired nothing so much as to bring evil to the Anunnaki. He flung his arms round Mummu, embraced and kissed him, and sat him on his knee so that they could whisper together their plans for the destruction of the gods.

But the spirits of the deep carried the whispers of evil to the ears of the Anunnaki, and Ea the all-wise saw even to the heart of the plot, and devised a counter-plot to prevent and overthrow it.

By the magic arts which his wisdom gave him he made a great spell, a charm that none can withstand, which is called Sleep. Ea spoke the charm, and the first Sleep floated across the waste of waters and fell upon Apsu. As soon as he was sleeping deeply, lying unguarded, drenched with slumber, and Mummu the adviser with him, Ea crept up to Apsu, took from him the crown of light which gave him his power, and placed it on his own head. Now Ea was all-powerful; and he speedily bound Apsu and slew him. He did not kill Mummu, but chained him to a rock and left him there.

Ea returned to the Halls of Heaven in triumph, and for a time there was peace between the old gods and the new. Ea dwelt in splendour with his wife Damkina; and their bedchamber was the room of the fates, the dwelling-place of the destinies—for there Bel Marduk, Marduk the Lord, was born.

When Ea saw his son the sight filled his heart with gladness, and he made haste to bestow on him all the gifts that were his to give. He made him perfect in beauty and strength, giving him a double godliness above all gods. His shape was perfect beyond words to express or thoughts to imagine, for he had four eyes and four ears—eyes that could see all things, and ears to hear every sound. When he opened his mouth fire issued from it, and he was taller than all the gods and shone more brightly, so that Damkina, speaking to him as a mother does to her child, called him 'My little son! My little Sun! Son of the heavens, heavenly Sun!'

When he was fully grown the Anunnaki set on his head the fiery crown as of ten gods; and Anu created the Four Winds to be his servants.

But now Tiamat grew really alarmed; and the old gods, the spirits of the deep, came to her and said:

'When these upstart gods slew Apsu your husband you raised no hand to help him. Now Anu has made the Four Winds to tear you asunder and give us no peace. Remember Apsu, and also Mummu the vanquished! Think of us, your true children, and of what we suffer! Give rest and avenge Apsu! Make war on the new gods, the Anunnaki, and destroy them utterly!'

Tiamat was pleased when she heard these words, and she made ready for battle, saying: 'Let us make monsters to smite these upstarts and devour them; let us do battle against the gods and destroy them!' And, when her forces were complete, Tiamat gathered them around her and they discussed their plans for the war.

But Ea knew what was happening; and he also held a council, calling all the Anunnaki together, and setting old Anshar his grandfather in the place of honour.

Then Ea stood before Anshar and said: 'Tiamat, to whom we all owe our being, detests us. She has gathered her council of the elder gods, and about her are the spirits of the deep, the Utukku. She is furious with rage, and they join in her anger and march at her side, plotting day and night to work us ill and bring us to destruction. They are ready for the battle and await us growling and raging.

'Worse than this, Tiamat herself has made new weapons and created terrible creatures to fight against us—monster serpents, sharp of tooth and deadly of fang; roaring dragons with flaming crowns as if they were gods: they lust for our blood and surely none can stand against them. For she sends out to fight us the Viper and the Dragon and the Sphinx, the Great Lion, the Mad Dog, and the Scorpion, mighty Lion demons, the Dragonfly and the Centaur. They are armed also with weapons that spare none. And over her forces she has set a new god whom she has made from the blood of Apsu, even Kingu who is now her lord. She has cast spells for Kingu, making him as powerful as ever Apsu was; she has hung the Tablets of Fate about his neck and promised him the power of Anu if he will destroy all the Anunnaki.'

When Anshar heard all this he was troubled indeed. He bit his lips and slapped his legs in despair.

'Surely you can slay Kingu!' he cried. 'You who killed Apsu and conquered Mummu!'

But Ea shook his head and drew back in fear.

Then Anshar the old turned to Anu his son and said: 'You, bravest of gods and heroes, whose strength nothing can resist: go up against Tiamat, slaughter Kingu. And if this may not be so, speak cunning words to Tiamat and see if peace can be made between the old gods and the new.'

Anu bowed to his father and set out at once towards where Tiamat was marshalling her forces. But when he saw her and understood all that she planned against him and his children, he was not able to face her, and turned back in fear to Anshar his father.

Anshar stared speechlessly at the ground for a while, his lips set firmly, and deep silence fell on the Anunnaki, as they thought to themselves: 'No god can face Tiamat in battle and escape with his life.'

At last Anshar rose in the assembly and said in solemn tones:

'I have pondered in my heart, and it comes to me that only one can save us now: Marduk the hero shall be our avenger.'

Ea sought out Marduk in his secret dwelling-place. 'Listen to my advice', he said, 'and heed it carefully. Come before Anshar ready for war; glare at him fiercely as if about to do battle. Do not kneel to him—stand on your feet. In this way you will show him that it is you whom he needs.'

Bel Marduk rejoiced at his father's words. He strode proudly into the presence of Anshar the old and stood in front of him, looking him straight in the eyes.

When Anshar saw him his heart was filled with joy. He kissed his mighty descendant, and the gloom passed from his heart.

'Anshar, be silent no longer!' cried Marduk. 'I will go and do all that you desire. I will go and slay Tiamat—yes, and trample Kingu under foot.'

'Go forth in your storm chariot, and conquer!' cried Anshar. 'Tiamat herself shall not be able to stand against you!'

'Maker of the gods,' said Bel Marduk, 'if I am to be the avenger, proclaim me now supreme among all the gods here in the great assembly. Let my word instead of yours determine fate; let all that I make be unchangeable, and all my commands be obeyed.'

Anshar gathered all the gods there were into the assembly and held a banquet in the Halls of Heaven. After the food they drank strong, sweet wine through the golden drinking-tubes, and as they drank their bodies swelled and they became languid and happy.

So they set Marduk willingly on the highest throne. 'Bel Marduk, from this day forth be the most honoured of the gods!' they cried. 'Unchangeable shall be your decrees: no god shall disobey you. Marduk, you are indeed our avenger, and we grant you kingship over the whole universe.'

Then they set a piece of cloth before Marduk and said: 'Bel Marduk, Marduk our lord, you are now the first of the gods. You have but to speak to destroy or to create. Speak the word, and this cloth shall vanish: speak again, and it shall be made whole once more.'

'Be destroyed!' cried Marduk, pointing at the cloth. And at once it decayed into dust and vanished completely.

'Be made again!' cried Marduk, and at once the dust drew together and grew into the piece of cloth which had been there before.

When the gods saw this they all cried aloud with one voice:
'Marduk is king!' Then they crowned him and clothed him in
royal robes, placing the sceptre in his hand. But afterwards they
returned him his armour and set weapons in his hands, saying:

'Go now and end the life of Tiamat. And may the winds carry
her blood into unknown places.'

Now that all power had been given to Marduk, he prepared
himself for the battle. First of all he invented the bow, making it
his special weapon and setting an arrow on the string, while others
hung in a quiver at his side. Then he took his mace and sprang
into his chariot, letting loose the lightning in front of him and
breathing it into his lungs until his whole body glowed as if with
fire. He made also a net in which to catch Tiamat, and he stationed
the Four Winds to hold her if she escaped.

Then he made seven new Winds, the Winds of Vengeance:
the Evil Wind and the Whirlwind, the Hurricane and the Cyclone,
the Fourfold Wind and the Sevenfold Wind and the Destroying
Wind. With these about him he raised the flood-storm, his secret
weapon, and sped over the roaring waters in his chariot of terror
to which was harnessed a team of four: the Killer, the Merciless,

the Trampler and the Swift. Their teeth were sharp, dripping with poison, and they were skilful in destruction and savagery.

Wrapped in the Cloak of Terror, Marduk urged his chariot towards Tiamat, a charm held firmly in his lips, and a plant to cure poison in his left hand. Behind him, but at a distance, came the warriors of the Anunnaki. But as he drew near the chariot swayed from side to side, and the Anunnaki paused, and looked on through a haze.

Tiamat uttered a terrible spell and howled her defiance. But Marduk held her with his secret weapon the flood-storm and cried out:

'Why have you risen against us, and given to Kingu the rank which was Apsu's? It can never be his! You seek evil against the gods—therefore I challenge you to single combat!'

When Tiamat heard this she went mad with rage. Her senses forsook her and she rushed upon him, casting her spells and smiting with her weapons. Marduk caught her in his net, and when she opened her mouth to devour him, he cast the Evil Wind down her throat so that she could not close her jaws upon him. While her mouth was open and her body stretched out by the Evil Wind, Marduk shot an arrow down her throat into her very heart.

Tiamat fell, and Marduk mounted in triumph on to her huge body, directing the battle until all her followers were slain or bound. He himself seized Kingu and loaded him with chains.

Then, the battle won, Marduk split Tiamat like a shellfish into two parts and of them made the sky and the earth of a new world, which was to become the world of man. He caused the sun and the moon to shine at their proper times—the sun to rise and set each day, and the moon to wax and wane in a month.

After this he held an assembly of the triumphant gods, and declared his plans to them:

'I will make a kind of savage who shall be called "Man"!' he said, 'and he and his kind shall dwell in the new world which I have made out of dead Tiamat. Mankind shall build temples and make sacrifices and do us worship.'

Then Ea said: 'Great Marduk, I will do the work of shaping Man. But my advice is that you mingle a little of the gods with him. Let one of the gods go into his making—a drop of the divine blood flow in his veins!'

Marduk answered: 'It shall be as you advise. And as Kingu led the war against us and encouraged Tiamat in her cruelty, it is only just that Kingu's blood should be shed for the making of Man.'

And so Man came into being in the Land of the Two Rivers, and the gods gave him Babylon and taught him to raise mighty temples in their honour.

Yet the evil blood of Kingu was too strong in the veins of the first race of men, and they soon turned to wickedness and forgot the gods. Then the Anunnaki were called together and it was decided to destroy mankind, who seemed to have disappointed his makers so sadly.

But Ea, he who had shaped the first men, was loath to see the work of his hands destroyed utterly. And he knew, even if fierce Marduk did not, that all men were not equally wicked. There was one man at least who was everything that he should be: this was Ziusudra, whom some call Utnapishtim, whose house of wood and reeds was set in the country at a little distance from the wicked city of Babylon.

Ea was determined to save him and his family. But all the Anunnaki had sworn a solemn oath to tell no living creature of the doom in store.

'I will tell no *living* creature,' thought Ea at length, 'but there is no reason why I should not speak my thoughts aloud to the trees and the reeds. . . . If Ziusudra happens to overhear, how can I help it?'

So he came by night to the house of Ziusudra and spoke to the wood and the reeds of which the walls were made:

'Reed hut, reed hut, listen to me! Walls of timber and reeds, pay good heed to my words! You are doomed, and nothing can save you, unless Ziusudra, the man who lives within you, is wise. If he pulls you down and makes you into a ship, you will be saved. He must make you into a great ship, as wide as she is long, with a roof to keep out the rain; and he must go into her with all his family, and with male and female of the beasts and the birds and the reptiles; and he must carry food for all who are in her for seven days and seven days more.'

When Ziusudra heard this he did not hesitate to obey the words of Ea. As soon as day came he set his whole family to work, and all his servants and the craftsmen who dwelt about his house. Even the children worked, carrying bitumen to seal and caulk the ship so that no drop of water should get in between the planks of her sides and bottom, or through the reeds with which she was thatched.

It was a great and wondrous ship, this ark of refuge which Ziusudra made. Her floor space was a whole acre, and there were six decks dividing her into seven parts, while there were nine rooms on each deck. She was sealed and caulked with bitumen that filled six huge measures each holding eight thousand gallons, with three measures of asphalt and one measure of oil. And the stores for those who were to sail in her were of salted beef and mutton, and wine both red and white.

On the seventh day the ship was completed, and with great toil and labour was launched on the broad stream of the River Euphrates—and even so, only two-thirds was in the water and the rest still deep in the mud of the bank.

When the people of Babylon asked Ziusudra what he was doing, he replied that he was going to sail on the Great Water, in search of a new home in a better land. At which they laughed and jeered at him, and returned to their wicked doings in the great city.

But Ziusudra took into his ship all his valuables of silver and gold, and all his family and relations; also the beasts of the field and the wild creatures of the woods and mountains; and last of all his servants and the craftsmen who had helped him to build his ark of refuge.

Scarcely were all aboard and the doors shut tight when the weather began to change. With the first glow of dawn a black cloud rose up from the horizon, and the thunder began to rumble and the lightning to flash. Then it seemed as if the king of the dead had torn out the posts which dammed back the waters under the earth: the water rose over the land, and the rain poured down from the black clouds which turned day into gloomy night, and the south wind blew so strongly that the flood was held from running down the Valley of the Two Rivers into the sea, so that the whole land was drowned with every living creature in it.

Even the gods turned their eyes away from the dreadful sight of the deluge, and Ishtar the goddess of love cried aloud in anguish, while Anu and Ea sat still and unmoving, their faces drawn, their lips close together—and Marduk shaded his eyes with his hand.

For six days and nights the waters rose and the south wind blew. But on the seventh day the wind ceased and the clouds melted away.

Ziusudra looked out from the ark and saw nothing but a waste of waters, a landscape as level as a flat roof. Then he sat and wept, knowing that all mankind other than those who were with him had returned to clay.

Now the ark began to move again; it came to rest on the top of Mount Nisir which appeared above the flood, and there it stuck fast. Ziusudra waited for seven days more, while the waters sank and sank all around him, and then he sent out a dove from the ark. Out went the dove, but it came back, since there was no resting-place for it. Then Ziusudra sent out a swallow; but it too returned since even it could not fly far enough to find dry land. Lastly Ziusudra sent out a raven, and the waters had fallen so far that he could find food; and he flew round cawing but did not return.

Then Ziusudra opened the door of the ark, and he and all that

were with him went out on to Mount Nisir. There Ziusudra
offered a great sacrifice to the gods, and in particular to Ea who
had saved him.

But when the god Enlil, who had caused the flood, saw that
Ziusudra and his household had escaped, he was filled with fury.

'A man is still alive on earth!' he cried in the assembly place
of the Anunnaki. 'And we decreed that no man was to escape
destruction!'

'Valiant Enlil,' said Ea smoothly, 'you did not think carefully
enough when you caused the deluge. Surely only the wicked were
to perish? You should have sent lions to diminish mankind,
instead of the flood! You should have sent packs of wolves, or a
famine or a pestilence: you would have done so, had you but
thought, and so diminished mankind without causing the flood.
As for Ziusudra, he saw our purposes in a dream, and now his
children and his household are alive to repeople the earth. And
now they have learned the power of the gods, and will not sin
against us as the first men did. Now they will go down into the
Valley of the Two Rivers and build cities by both Tigris and
Euphrates; and Babylon shall rise again to bring us glory.'

At this Enlil was satisfied; and the Anunnaki praised Ea; and
Marduk caused all that he had said to come to pass.

But Ziusudra and his wife they made immortal, and took them
to dwell in Dilmun, the Garden of the Sun, the Land of the Living
where the raven utters no cries, and there is neither sickness nor
death. The lion does not snatch away the kid for food in Dilmun,
nor the hawk swoop on the dove, nor is there any sorrow or sin.
And there for ever dwells Ziusudra the Faraway: but it seems that
to him alone of the sons of men did the Anunnaki, the gods of
Babylon, give everlasting life.

Tammuz and Ishtar

Besides Ishtar, the goddess of love, Anu had another daughter called Ereshkigal, who became queen of Kur, the Land of No Return where the dead dwell—for Anu gave it to her after the slaying of Apsu when he became lord of the sky and his brother Enlil ruled over the earth.

Ereshkigal felt that she had been driven out by the gods of Heaven and earth, and she grew to hate them, even after mankind had been created, and she had plenty of subjects in her dark and miserable realm.

The gods, the Anunnaki, knew this, and to show her how highly they honoured her they prepared a banquet in the Halls of Heaven, at which she was to be the guest—and so the queen of the feast.

They sent a messenger to her to invite her, who said: 'The Anunnaki bid me say that although they cannot come down to Kur to visit you, it is easy for you to come up to them. Therefore come with speed, for a great feast is prepared in your honour.'

Ereshkigal was suspicious, and she sent up her vizier, her chief adviser, who was called Namtar, to see if the invitation was in earnest, or whether the Anunnaki meant to mock her.

Namtar came to the Halls of Heaven, and the gods greeted the messenger of their mighty sister with all the honour that was due. Only one of them, a minor god called Nergal, failed to do proper reverence to the messenger from Kur.

Namtar told Ereshkigal of this, and she sent him back to the Anunnaki to say:

'Ereshkigal, queen of the Land of No Return, will come to your banquet if you hand over to her the god who did not rise and show proper respect to my messenger. Him I will slay and tear into pieces. Then I will come to the banquet in the Halls of Heaven.'

The Anunnaki greeted Namtar kindly, and when he delivered his message they said:

'Look for the god who did not rise up when you came before, and if you can find him take him to your mistress.'

Namtar counted the gods, and at first he could not find the one for whom he was seeking. But Nergal was so frightened that he began to snivel in his place of hiding behind the rest of the Anunnaki, and Namtar knew that here was the one.

'Return to your mistress,' said Anu, 'and tell her that we will send Nergal to her in due time.'

When Namtar had gone, Nergal came weeping to his father Ea, Anu's mighty son, and said:

'When Ereshkigal sees me, she will take away my life and tear me in pieces!'

'Do not be afraid,' said Ea. 'I will give you seven demons, and then seven more, and they shall go with you and protect you against Ereshkigal!'

So Nergal set out bravely with his fourteen followers, the deadly demons of disease, and came to the outer gate of Kur.

'Gatekeeper, open!' he cried. 'Ereshkigal has sent for me, and I am here!'

'There is a certain god, one of the Anunnaki, standing at the entrance and asking for our Queen Ereshkigal,' reported the gatekeeper to Namtar.

When Namtar saw that it was Nergal he hastened to his mistress, and she cried:

'Bring him in! When he comes I will slay him, and tear him to pieces!'

'Enter, my lord, into the house of Ereshkigal!' said Namtar, as the first gate was opened to Nergal.

But no victim came in to his death—rather a warrior to capture Kur. For Nergal placed two demons on guard at each gate that he passed, and then cut down the wardens at the door of Ereshkigal's palace, crying: 'The city is ours! Follow me, demons!'

He rushed into the hall where Ereshkigal sat on her throne, the demons behind him, and caught her by the hair, his sword held on high:

'Do not smite me, noble Nergal!' cried Ereshkigal in terror. 'Let me speak a word! Be my husband, and I will marry you willingly. And I will make you king of Kur, of the Land of No Return, and of all who dwell in it. You shall be its master, even as I am its mistress.'

When Nergal heard these words he flung down his sword, kissed Ereshkigal and wiped away her tears, saying:

'In spite of the fate you had planned for me, I will marry you and let all be as you said.'

So Ereshkigal and Nergal became king and queen of the dead, with the demons of disease as their servants to bring them new subjects.

After this Ereshkigal and her husband feasted with the Anunnaki, and there was peace between them—but no love. For of all the Anunnaki only Nergal visited Kur and remained alive, and indeed there was no desire on the part of any of the others to seek the dread path to the dark regions below or to pass the Seven Gates of Kur.

But Ereshkigal wandered on the earth when she wished, and often her sister Ishtar went as her companion.

But there was little love between the sisters of life and death, and what there was turned to bitter hatred when Tammuz was born.

About his birth there was a mystery. His father was the god Ningishzida, lord of the Wood of Life; but before he was born his mother turned herself into a tree to escape from the demons who were pursuing her. When the time of his birth arrived the trunk of the tree split open, and the baby Tammuz fell from it.

Ishtar found the child and would have brought him up. But the Anunnaki decreed that for half of each year he should be entrusted to Ereshkigal. So, until he was fully grown, Tammuz spent half of each year above the ground and the other half below it.

Tammuz grew into the most beautiful of all the gods, and both Ishtar and Ereshkigal loved him. When he was grown, however, Tammuz chose to dwell above the ground with Ishtar, and for a time they were supremely happy together, and all earth smiled in such a summer as was never seen before or since: a summer such as that which makes of Dilmun an eternal Paradise.

Among the trees and flowers wandered Tammuz and Ishtar in their perfect happiness: hunting the wild beasts for sport, or sitting and singing under the shadow of a tree on the grassy hillside.

Yet there was a shadow over their happiness darker than that which any tree could cast; for both knew that Ereshkigal would not forgive.

Tammuz was a god and could not be killed in any ordinary way. Yet while he dwelt on earth a god stronger than he could slay him. Ereshkigal knew this, and at length she set a snare for Tammuz.

Ishtar had guarded him round with charms and spells so that

not only could no mortal creature harm him, but if any god drew near to him she would know and come to his protection.

But Ereshkigal turned Nergal into a great wild boar and sent him to wait his chance in the woods above the city of Babylon where Tammuz hunted.

Ishtar had grown careless, since so long had passed and Ereshkigal had made no move to injure or capture Tammuz; and when she saw him chasing a wild boar among the trees she thought it was no more than a common beast whom he delighted to hunt.

Suddenly, however, the boar which was Nergal turned and attacked Tammuz. His spear leapt back from its shoulder without so much as grazing it, but a moment later the boar was upon Tammuz and had wounded him deeply in the thigh with its sharp curved tusk.

Tammuz lay bleeding on the ground, and Ishtar, her cries of grief echoing among the mountains, sped to him and knelt at his side.

All through the long summer day she wept beside him, striving to staunch the blood; and the women of Babylon wept also for dying Tammuz, as they were to weep each year at the summer's ending in memory of his death.

As Tammuz died the leaves and grasses turned brown and died also, and when night fell and death took him there was winter all over the earth.

Ishtar knew that now Tammuz was dead he must dwell for ever in Kur, the Land of No Return, and that Ereshkigal had won him. But she was determined not to lose her lover without a struggle and so, arming herself with every charm she knew, Ishtar set off to the lower world. Before she went, however, she left instructions with her faithful servant the messenger Ninshubur:

'I am now descending to the world beneath. If I do not return after three days, fill Heaven with lamentations for me: put on sackcloth, scratch your cheeks, dim your eyes with tears, and go to the gods, the Anunnaki—and last of all to Enlil and Anu and Ea and beg them to bring me out of the power of Ereshkigal. Go, Ninshubur; do not neglect to do all that I command.'

Then Ishtar set out for the Land of No Return, the dark house of Ereshkigal, the place which none leaves who has entered it, by the dark road on which there is no way back.

When she came to the outermost gate of Kur, she cried:

'Gatekeeper, open the gate so that I may enter! Open with speed, or I will smash the door, I will shatter the bolt, I will break the posts and cause the lintel to fall!'

'Wait awhile, lady of love!' cried Neti the gatekeeper. 'I will tell your sister Ereshkigal that you are here.'

When Ereshkigal heard that Ishtar stood at the gate, her face turned pale with hatred and her lips set in an evil smile.

'Open the gates to Ishtar my sister,' she commanded. 'Let her enter by the dark road on which there is no way back; let her come into the Land of No Return.'

Back sped Neti the gatekeeper to open the door for her, saying:

'Enter, my lady, so that Kur may rejoice over you, so that the Land of No Return may be glad at your presence.'

As Ishtar came through the first gate the keeper took away the great crown from her head.

'Gatekeeper, why do you take away my crown?' asked Ishtar.

'Enter, my lady,' was all he answered, 'for such are the rules of the Mistress of the Lower World.'

As Ishtar passed through the second gate he took away the pendants from her ears.

'Gatekeeper, why do you take away my pendants?' asked Ishtar.

'Enter, my lady,' he answered, 'for such are the rules of the Mistress of the Lower World.'

As she went through the third gate he lifted the chains from about her neck.

'Gatekeeper, why do you take my necklaces?' asked Ishtar.

'Enter, my lady, for such are the rules of the Mistress of the Lower World.'

As she entered the fourth gateway he loosed the golden breast-plates that she wore.

'Gatekeeper, why do you rob me of my breast ornaments?' asked Ishtar.

'Enter, my lady,' was all he would say, 'for such are the rules of the Mistress of the Lower World.'

As she crossed the threshold of the fifth gateway he stripped the girdle of birth-stones from about her hips.

'Gatekeeper, why do you loose the girdle of birth-stones from about my waist?' asked Ishtar.

'Enter, my lady, for such are the rules of the Mistress of the Lower World,' he repeated.

As she was led through the sixth gateway he unfastened the clasps from about her wrists and ankles.

'Gatekeeper, why do you unfasten my clasps?' asked Ishtar.

'Enter, my lady,' he said, 'for such are the rules of the Mistress of the Lower World.'

Now they came to the last gateway, which was the door of the great hall of Kur; and here the gatekeeper took from Ishtar her last adornment.

'Gatekeeper, why have you stripped me even of my jewelled loincloth?' she asked.

'Enter, my lady,' said he for the last time, 'for such are the rules of the Mistress of the Lower World.'

Thus Ishtar came all naked into the presence of Ereshkigal, the queen of the dead, and stood before her throne.

When she saw her Ereshkigal taunted her with such bitter, evil words that Ishtar flew at her in fury. At once the demons of Kur leapt upon her and held her back, and Ereshkigal said with a smile of triumph:

'Go, Namtar, and take this dead woman to the place prepared for her, hang her there and set loose to prey upon her the Sixty Miseries; set the Misery of the Eyes against her eyes, and the Misery of the Sides against her sides, and the Misery of the Heart against her heart, and every Misery against every part of her body.'

So Ishtar was given over to the tormentors, and her corpse was hung from a stake driven into the wall, and she was as a dead woman and could do nothing.

After three days and three nights had passed her faithful servant Ninshubur the messenger filled Heaven and earth with his lamentations, scratched his face, put on sackcloth and with tears running from his eyes went from one of the Anunnaki to another, saying:

'Mighty lords, let not Ishtar be put to death in the Lower World. Let not her beauty be marred as if lapis lazuli were broken up to pack a wall with instead of useless stones. Ishtar has gone down to the Lower World and has not returned; she has gone to the Land of No Return and the world is left desolate. Love has gone and sweet desire: now there are no more marriages, no children are born, the beasts and the birds do not mate with one another, and soon the world will be empty because Ishtar the lady of love and life has left it.'

All the Anunnaki grieved, but not one of them could do anything to save Ishtar.

At last Ninshubur came to Ea, and that great god sent down his own newly created messenger Asushunamur bearing both gifts and promises to Ereshkigal—but also threats and commands which she dared not disobey. For Ea told her that Ishtar must return to earth lest the whole world come to ruin, and that, if she did not obey, Marduk the avenger would come against her even, as he had come against Tiamat in the great war of the gods.

So Ereshkigal caused Ishtar to be cut down from the stake and brought before her. And, in the great hall of the dead, Asushunamur poured the water of life over Ishtar, and Ereshkigal promised to send Tammuz back to earth for half of every year.

Ishtar went from before Ereshkigal by the Seven Gates of Kur, and at the seventh gate her jewelled loincloth was returned to her, at the sixth her clasps, at the fifth her girdle, at the fourth her breastplates, at the third her necklaces, at the second her ear pendants and at the outer gate her shining crown.

Meanwhile Ereshkigal said to Namtar:

'Bring Tammuz whom she loves and wash him with the water of life. Anoint him with sweet oil, clothe him with a red garment, and give him his flute of shining blue lapis lazuli.'

Scarcely had Ishtar reached the Upper World when she heard the notes of the flute drawing near behind her, and knew that it was Tammuz her beloved.

Then she laughed aloud for joy, and at once the earth seemed to laugh with her. The bare ground turned green with the swiftly growing corn; the bare branches burgeoned suddenly with new green leaves, the flowers budded and blossomed.

And with the spring, as Tammuz and Ishtar wandered hand in hand through the world, love was born again in the hearts of man and maid, and among all living creatures.

But when the time came for Tammuz to return to Ereshkigal, Ishtar wept once more, and the women of Babylon wept with her, while autumn came swiftly over the earth and bleak winter followed—until spring came once more as Tammuz came piping up the dark road from Kur in search of Ishtar his love.

The Adventures of Gilgamesh

T HE EARLIEST kings of Babylon were children of the gods,
yet though they were stronger and more powerful than
any man since their day, even they were mortal and at last
died and went to the realm of Ereshkigal to lie in darkness and
feed on mud.

Two of these kings, who were almost gods, tried to win immortality. The first of them was Adapa, whose home was in the city of
Eridu, near where the River Euphrates ran out into the sea.

Adapa was a great fisherman, and each day he sailed out into
the Persian Gulf to fish. One day, however, the South Wind rose

suddenly, upset his boat, and sent him to the Land of Fishes at the bottom of the sea.

'South Wind!' cried Adapa in anger. 'I will punish you for treating me like this! I will break your wing, so that you can blow no more!'

So saying Adapa the all-wise spoke a great charm, and the South Wind fell from the sky, his wing broken.

Presently Anu called to his vizier, Ilabrat: 'Why has the South Wind not blown over the land for seven days?'

'My lord,' answered Ilabrat, 'Adapa the son of Ea has broken the wing of the South Wind.'

'Bring him before me!' commanded Anu, and Ilabrat set out for the Land of Fishes.

But Ea heard the words of Anu, and he went in haste to Adapa his wise son and told him what he must do. 'And be sure that if Anu offers you food and drink you touch neither,' ended Ea. 'For they will be the bread and water of death which will bring you at once to the Land of No Return, to Kur where Ereshkigal is queen.'

Adapa dressed himself in sackcloth like one who mourns; he scratched his cheeks, and the tears ran from his eyes. When Ilabrat brought him to the great door of the Hall of Heaven in which Anu sat to give judgment, two gods were standing on guard: Tammuz and his father Ningishzida.

'Man, for whom do you mourn?' they asked.

'I mourn for the two gods who perished upon the earth,' answered Adapa. 'For Tammuz who makes green the earth in spring, and Ningishzida, lord of the Wood of Life.'

When the two gods heard this they were well pleased, and they said:

'Come with us, man, and we will lead you to Anu and plead for you.'

So they led him before Anu and spoke so persuasively of the wisdom and virtue of Adapa, pointing out that the South Wind was entirely to blame for what had happened, that Anu's heart was changed. Not only did he forgive Adapa, but he decided to

honour him as only one other man, Ziusudra, had been honoured.
Instead of the bread and water of death, he sent for the bread and
water of life, and offered them to Adapa. This was a thing which
Ea, for all his wisdom, never dreamt might happen, and Adapa,
still obeying his commands, refused to eat and drink and so missed
his chance of immortality for ever.

Gilgamesh the mighty king of Erech also set out to seek for
eternal life. No king so mighty ever ruled over Babylon, nor one
who, though mortal, was more of a god. He was so strong and
powerful that no one could stand against him or even equal him,
and the people of Babylon prayed to the gods, saying:

'Create a companion for Gilgamesh and send them forth to do
mighty deeds. He is as strong as a wild bull, the master of the
herd—and like a bull he takes from us our daughters and our
sweethearts when he wishes to add them to his harem, and we
cannot stop him.'

'This is your doing,' said Anu to the goddess Aruru. 'Gilgamesh is your child. You have made him too mighty to live
among men. Make another like him who will lead him to seek
feats of strength and far quests.'

Aruru took clay, fashioned it in the form of Anu himself and
bade Ninurta the son of Enlil breathe life into this new man.

The stranger upon the earth was called Enkidu. His body was
shaggy with hair; he did not know that he was a man, but ran
wild with the beasts of the field. His friends were the gazelles; with
them he ate grass and with them jostled at the watering-place.
He sought out and filled up the pits and traps which the hunters
had made for his friends; and the hunters were afraid of him and
fled far from their usual haunts.

They came to Erech and told Gilgamesh of all they had seen.
'Come against this wild man,' they said. 'Only you are strong
enough to overcome him.'

Gilgamesh laughed. 'He can be conquered by a woman,' he
said, and chose the fairest of the priestesses of Ishtar. 'Go to
Enkidu,' he told her, 'and charm him with your beauty. Once he
is yours he will run with the beasts no more.'

The girl did as Gilgamesh bade her, and when Enkidu saw her he forgot all else but her beauty. For six days and seven nights he dwelt with her. Then he grew restless and longed for his old life among the beasts. So he set off for the watering-place running to greet his friends the gazelles. But when they saw him they snorted in terror and ran away from him as they would from any human.

Then Enkidu knew that he was no longer a brother of the wild things, but a man as other men are. So he returned to the girl who had won him, and said to her:

'Take me to the city where Gilgamesh dwells. I will show him that I am mightier, and seize it for myself.'

Enkidu came to Erech, and there Gilgamesh met him and they wrestled together, shaking the earth like two young bulls each anxious to rule the herd. For several rounds neither was the victor; but both stood back at last almost exhausted.

As they looked at one another hate died out of their hearts and love came to take its place. So they clasped hands and became closer than brothers: never was there a friendship like that of Gilgamesh and Enkidu.

Now they sat together as kings in Erech, clad in gorgeous robes and wearing crowns of gold. All the lesser kings knelt before them and kissed their feet, and the people of Erech honoured them equally.

But after a while strange dreams began to trouble the slumbers of both Gilgamesh and Enkidu, and ghastly visions of the Land of No Return where the dead lie eating mud in the darkness over which Ereshkigal rules.

Gilgamesh sought the advice of Shamash, the Wind-god, who told him to set out with Enkidu to seek for the Cedar Mountain which was guarded by the giant Khumbaba. Enkidu was loath to go for his heart told him that evil and sorrow would come to them both. But Gilgamesh would not be turned from his quest; he was eager to fight the giant Khumbaba, the Demon of the Cedar Mountain, and show that he was greater even than such a monster.

Long and perilous was their journey; twenty thousand hours it took them to reach the foot of the Cedar Mountain.

At last they stood and gazed at the forest of cedars, at the great height of the trees, at the wide path made by the giant feet of Khumbaba. The whole mountain was covered with cedars, sweet-smelling and shady; it was a paradise fit for the abode of any god or goddess—and indeed, as they were to learn, it was the chosen dwelling-place of Ishtar the goddess of love and beauty.

Gilgamesh strode into the forest and called for Khumbaba to come and fight him. But there was no sign of the Demon of the Cedar Mountain.

'Let us turn away while there is still time,' begged Enkidu. 'Evil awaits us here, and my hands seem weak and my legs paralysed.'

Gilgamesh was not to be turned, however. He strode into the forest until he came to a great clearing, and here he took his axe and began to cut down one of the cedar trees.

When Khumbaba heard the sound of the axe he roared with fury, and his voice shook the forest like the breath of a tempest.

'Who dares to cut down a tree on my cedar mountain?' he howled, and at once he came rushing to do battle with Gilgamesh.

'Now help me, Shamash!' Gilgamesh cried as he drew his sword. And the Wind-god helped with such good will that soon Khumbaba was blown from his feet and Gilgamesh sprang upon him and cut off his head.

After this Enkidu and Gilgamesh bathed in the stream and clothed themselves in fair clean garments. Then they wandered in the beautiful forest, and their hearts were filled with joy and peace.

But Ishtar saw Gilgamesh, and at once she fell in love with him. So she came to him in all her divine beauty and met him in a forest glade, saying:

'Come, Gilgamesh, and be my lover. You shall be my husband and I will be your wife; and I will harness for you a chariot of lapis and gold, with wheels also of gold and rails of brass. You shall have storm-demons to draw it instead of mules, and our house shall be fragrant with cedar.'

Gilgamesh did not fall to the false lures of Ishtar, however.

'How can I be a husband to a goddess?' he asked. 'Moreover I know well that no good has ever come to any whom you have loved. What of Tammuz, your first beloved? Do not the women of Babylon wail for him year after year, while he dwells in sorrow among the shades in Kur? What of your lover whom you turned into a bird when you were tired of him, and broke his wing with a stone? Did you not turn another into a lion and dig seven pits for him? Was not one turned into a wolf and torn to pieces by the hounds? And what of Ishullanu, whom you changed into a mole and doomed to dwell for ever eating his way through the earth?'

When Ishtar heard this she went away in a whirlwind of rage and sent the Bull of Heaven to slay him. But Gilgamesh tore off its tail, which he flung in Ishtar's face; and the Bull itself he cast up into the sky to shine for ever as the constellation of *Taurus*.

Realizing that she could do nothing to harm Gilgamesh, cruel Ishtar cast a spell on Enkidu instead. For twelve days he lay ill, and nothing that Gilgamesh could do helped him in any way; and on the thirteenth day he died in Gilgamesh's arms.

When Enkidu was dead, panic seized Gilgamesh: 'Let me flee away through the land!' he cried. 'Enkidu is dead, my friend, my dear brother, who chased the panther of the desert, who killed lions at my side—he is dead! Six days and six nights I have wept over him. Now I am afraid of death and must flee from it. My friend whom I loved has become no more than stinking mud. Must I lie one day as he lies, never to rise again?'

The fear of death was so strong upon Gilgamesh that he decided to leave his home and his kingdom and wander out in quest of immortality. If anyone could help him to find it, that one was Ziusudra, the only man ever to be made immortal, after he had survived the flood.

Gilgamesh set out in search of Ziusudra the Faraway who dwelt for ever in Dilmun, beyond the Garden of the Sun. For a long time he could find no one who knew the road; but at last he came to the mountain of Mashu where every evening the Sun goes to rest. The entrance was guarded by scorpion-men so terrible to behold that even Gilgamesh was afraid at first.

Summoning up his courage, however, he spoke to the scorpion-guards, saying:

'Tell me, I beg you, how I may find Ziusudra. I wish to speak with him about life and death.'

'Gilgamesh, you in whose veins flows the blood of the gods,' answered the scorpion-man, 'Let me warn you that no mortal will ever achieve immortality. But if you insist on seeking Ziusudra, you must pass through this mountain by the road which leads for twelve leagues of utter darkness.'

'Whether in sorrow or in pain, in cold or in heat, sighing or weeping, still I will go forward,' declared Gilgamesh. 'Therefore, open the mountain, I beg of you.'

So Gilgamesh passed through the mountain and came with the dawn to the shores of the sea beside which, at the world's very end, was the Garden of the Sun. Here, among the trees of the gods which grew jewels instead of fruit, he met the goddess Siduri, who told him that Ziusudra lived still farther away, on an island across the Waters of Death.

'Urshanabi the boatman will take you over', she said, 'if you can punt the boat without allowing one drop of water to touch you. If one drop splashes on your hand or runs down the pole and touches you, you will fall dead—and Ereshkigal will claim you as hers.'

When Urshanabi arrived in his boat he took pity on Gilgamesh and told him to cut in the forest a hundred and twenty poles, each ninety feet long. With these Gilgamesh punted the boat, using each only once and leaving it behind him. In this way he came to the island without a drop of water touching his hands.

On the island of Dilmun he found Ziusudra, who asked why he had come.

'I have wandered over all lands,' answered Gilgamesh. 'I have climbed the mountains, I have crossed the seas. When my clothes wore out I slew tigers, stags and ibex and clothed myself in their skins. And all this I did to seek you, the Faraway, the Undying, to learn how I too may never die.'

'All men must die,' answered Ziusudra. 'Do we build a house

to last for ever? Does anything last for ever? Since the beginning all things have been but passing shadows. The sleeping and the dead are alike—for sleep is but the likeness of death. The king and the poor man are equal when the Anunnaki have ruled that their day is done.'

Ziusudra could do nothing to help Gilgamesh, for his own immortality had been given by the gods. Yet in the end he told him of a magic plant that grew at the bottom of the sea which was called 'Man Becomes Young in Old Age'.

'It will not make you immortal,' said Ziusudra. 'But it will renew your youth if you eat of it.'

So, at Ziusudra's command, Urshanabi the boatman rowed Gilgamesh to the place in the sea beneath which the magic plant grew. Gilgamesh tied heavy stones to his feet and sank to the bottom of the sea. There grew the plant, and in spite of its sharp thorns Gilgamesh tore off a branch before he cut the stones from his feet and shot up to the surface once more.

Then Urshanabi landed him, and he set out for Erech carrying the precious plant with him. All day he walked, and at night lay down to sleep beside a well of clear water. He was hot and tired after his day's journey in the sun, so he took off his clothes and plunged into the cool water. And while he was there a serpent came and carried off the magic plant down into the depths of the well. But as it went its old skin fell off, and it became young once more.

Gilgamesh sat weeping by the well. 'For whom have my hands toiled?' he sobbed. 'For whom has my heart's blood been spent? I have brought no blessing on myself after all my wanderings— all I have done is to give fresh youth to the serpents of the earth!'

So Gilgamesh's quest for immortality proved as vain as Adapa's had been. Sadly he returned to Erech, and lived out his days there as a good and mighty king whom his people loved and honoured, and whose name was remembered for ever after.

And when the end of his life came, Gilgamesh died as all men must, and went to seek his friend Enkidu in the dark and cheerless realm of Ereshkigal, the Land of No Return.

HITTITE

Lost Telepinu

THE HITTITES believed in many gods, though when they wrote of them their names were usually hidden by signs of which the priests alone knew the meaning, so we can only guess it in most cases.

As they lived on the southern slopes of the great mountains to the north of Palestine and Babylonia, the Hittites thought of Taru the Storm-god as one of the greatest powers of Heaven. For he brought the tempests down from the mountains, and the great floods too. But his son Telepinu was every bit as powerful, since he saw to it that when his father sent rain and gentle floods the seeds grew in the earth, the fruits formed on the trees, and all living creatures produced their young.

Hannahannas the great Sun-god had also to be favourable so that the crops and fruits should ripen in due season; and Inaras, queen of Heaven, was needed too so that love and desire might wake in the hearts of man and woman, and also of male and female among the beasts and birds.

The great enemy of the gods was Illuyankas the dragon, in whom was all evil. Often and often he tried to destroy mankind, and the fair earth which the gods had made, but always they were ready to defend it and drive him back.

Yet once he almost conquered. For Taru the Storm-god went

up against him alone and, after a great battle, Illuyankas defeated him and robbed him of his heart and eyes.

Then there was sorrow in heaven and despair upon earth. The gods could do nothing against Illuyankas the dragon for fear that he should destroy the eyes and heart of Taru, leaving the Storm-god sightless and heartless for ever.

Taru thought and thought; and at last he hit upon a device. Taking on the likeness of a man, he descended to earth and lived there in disguise until a woman, the daughter of a poor man, took pity on his blindness and became his wife.

This strange couple had one son, half human and half divine, who grew up to be a great hero among men. But not even he knew that his father was Taru the Storm-god. Illuyankas the dragon did not know either; but he saw a way of getting even more power over mankind—which was precisely what Taru had thought and hoped that he would do.

The dragon Illuyankas had a beautiful daughter, and he sent her to visit the handsome human son of Taru and the poor man's daughter. The young hero fell in love with the divine being; and, hoping also to win more power by marrying her, he asked her to be his wife.

She consented at once and, much to the delight of both divine fathers—though for very different reasons—the marriage was fixed.

But before the ceremony Taru, still disguised as a blind man, said to his son:

'Since you are marrying a daughter of Illuyankas, who is a sort of goddess, you must be very careful that she does not have everything her own way. If she does, she is certain to cast you off or even kill you as soon as she grows tired of you. Her father has not yet given you any marriage portion; go to him and remind him of this. And when he asks what you want, say: 'The heart and eyes of Taru the Storm-god.' Bring them to me, and I will show you how you may use them in such a way that you will become far more powerful than your wife—perhaps greater even than your father-in-law.'

Off went the young man to talk matters over with Illuyankas the dragon; and that monster, thinking that the more powerful his human son-in-law became, the stronger ally he would have against Taru and the gods, gave him the heart and eyes of the Storm-god without any hesitation.

As soon as Taru had his eyes and heart again he went to Kamrusepas, the goddess of magic and healing, and she soon restored them to their rightful places and made Taru as clear of vision and as high of heart as he had been before his battle with the dragon.

When Illuyankas saw how he had been tricked he was furious, but he decided to use guile instead of force in his next attempt, and so proposed a treaty of peace with the gods.

Taru agreed to this, and the gods invited Illuyankas and all his family to a great feast. The dragon accepted the invitation, for he felt that he was strong enough to defend himself and his children if any treachery was intended.

Meanwhile Taru went to Inaras, the queen of Heaven, and said:
'Lady of beauty, come to my aid! Help me by making the feast; but mix strong wines and spirits so that we may overcome the dragon once and for all.'

Inaras agreed; but so that the power of earth should be joined with the power of Heaven in the brewing of the drink, she clad herself in the shape of a mortal maiden, went down to Zigaratta in the land of the Hittites, and took a man named Hupasiyas to be her lover.

As soon as they were wed she told him who she really was, and took him with her to her palace in the sky. 'Here you may live for ever, both young and handsome—and my beloved,' she said. 'But there is one thing you must remember: you must never open the shutter and look out of the window down into the world of men.'

Then Inaras and Hupasiyas brewed sweet wine, and the strong spirit called by the Hittites *marnuwan*, and a stronger spirit still called *walhi*.

When all the wine-jars were filled to the brim, Inaras had them carried to the hall where the gods were holding the feast.

As soon as Illuyankas the dragon and his children arrived the great banquet began. They and the gods ate and drank until all the dishes and all the wine-jars were empty. Now the dragon and his family had never tasted wine and spirits before; and the result was that when the feast was ended they all fell on the floor dead drunk and could not move.

Then Taru drew his sword and killed the dragon Illuyankas, while the other gods did the same for his children. After this

Illuyankas and his family dwelt below the earth in the land of the dead, and could harm the gods no further; but they could still lead men into ill doing, coming among them as ghosts and demons, and whispering to them in their dreams.

While this was happening Hupasiyas dwelt alone in the palace of Inaras, waiting for her to return. When twenty days had gone by he could resist no longer the temptation to open the shutter and look through the window.

When he did so he saw Zigaratta below him, and his own house, and in front of it his wife and children. Inaras had taken from him all memory of them; but when he saw them his memory returned, and as soon as Inaras came back he fell at her feet crying: 'Let me go home!'

'You have opened the shutter and looked out of the window!' said Inaras. 'Now you must die like any other mortal.' So saying, she threw him out of Heaven, and that was the end of him.

But there was one god who had not been consulted over the means of tricking Illuyankas the dragon to restore the heart and eyes of Taru, or even of making him drunk at the feast of Inaras— and this was Telepinu, the son of Taru.

When he found that Taru had married a mortal and had a son who had become the greatest of heroes and won back his father's heart and eyes, Telepinu was so furious, and so filled with jealousy, that he decided to leave heaven for ever.

In a blind rage, madly cramming his left foot into his right shoe and his right foot into his left, he set out across the world. On and on he went until he was lost among the towering mountains far north of the land of the Hittites. Here, when at last he grew tired, Telepinu lay down to rest. Sleep came upon him, and he slept and slept until it seemed that he would never wake again.

As soon as Telepinu was gone from Heaven, want began to spread over the earth. No more babies were born, nor did the sheep have lambs nor the cows calve. The grass shrivelled, the trees put forth no green shoots, and pastures withered away and the springs dried up.

When he realized what was happening on earth, Hannahannas

the Sun-god called all the gods together for a great feast. But when they sat down, the food no longer satisfied their hunger nor did the wine quench their thirst.

'It is because Telepinu my son is not here,' said Taru. 'He has flown into a rage because of what I did, and has left Heaven; and every good thing has gone with him.'

The gods searched for Telepinu, but none of them could find him.

Then Hannahannas the Sun-god called the eagle to him and said: 'Go and seek for Telepinu. Search every mountain, however high, every valley, however dark, and every sea, however deep.'

Over all the earth went the eagle; but at length he returned to Hannahannas saying: 'I cannot find him. I cannot find Telepinu, the noble god.'

'What shall we do?' asked Taru the Storm-god. 'If we do not find Telepinu we shall die of hunger.'

'It is for you to search now,' said Hannahannas, and Taru the Storm-god set out, raging over all the earth. He blew open the gates of every city, and he blew in the doors of every house—but still there was no sign of Telepinu.

Then Taru the wise said to Hannahannas: 'The great gods and the lesser gods have searched for Telepinu, but they cannot find him. The eagle cannot find him on the mountains and in the wild places, nor can I discover him among the cities of men. But now I will send out one little bee who can go everywhere; perhaps it will prove cleverer than us all.'

'Send out the bee,' exclaimed Hannahannas, and Taru instructed it, saying: 'Go and search for Telepinu. When you find him, sting him on the hands and on the feet, so that the eagle may hear his cries.'

Away went the bee and searched by the flowing rivers and the murmuring springs. It had come to the end of both the honey and the wax which it carried, when at last it found Telepinu asleep in a meadow, hidden by the dark grove of Lihzina. At once it stung him on the hands and feet, and Telepinu woke, crying:

'I came here to be alone and enjoy my rage. How dare you wake me like this?'

Then the stings began to hurt him, and he cried aloud in pain and fury, so that the eagle who was hovering above heard him and swooped down.

'Take me to Kamrusepas, the goddess of healing!' said Telepinu, mounting on the eagle's back. The great bird spread its wings and away they went.

When they reached the beautiful spring called Hattara on the sacred mountain of Ammuna, Kamrusepas was waiting for him. 'Telepinu,' she said gently, 'here is the sweet and soothing essence of cedar. Here is ointment with which I will anoint the stings on your hands and feet. But let me also anoint your heart with it, so that the rage and fury may go from it even as the pain departs from your hands and feet. See, I draw forth the stings from them: tell me of the stings in your heart so that I may draw them forth also.'

Then Telepinu told her all, and she explained what Taru had done and why, so that the rage and jealousy died out of Telepinu's heart just as the pain of the stings faded from his hands and feet.

Kamrusepas left him by her sacred spring and hastened to the Halls of Heaven, where the gods still sat discussing how to find lost Telepinu.

She stood before them and said: 'Telepinu is found. And now I have taken away the pain from his body. I have also taken away the anger and the fury and the malice and the jealousy from his heart.'

After this Telepinu returned to his own place in the Halls of Heaven, and there was great rejoicing.

On earth there was more rejoicing still. For he cared once more for the land: he let the sheep feed on the hillsides once more, and the cattle in the meadows. The mother tended her child, the ewe tended her lamb, the cow tended her calf.

But ever after when winter came and it seemed that Telepinu was angry once more and had left the earth, the people of the Hittites hung the fleece of a sheep before the temple of Telepinu in token of the plenty for which they prayed—of corn and fruit and cattle and sheep in the coming spring—and sang:

'Oh, Telepinu, when you left the earth at the end of summer the green things withered and the ox grew thin, and the sheep also. Oh, Telepinu, cease from anger, cast away thy rage, and be kind to us.

'Away with the fury and malice from the heart of Telepinu. Drive them out of the house, out of the window, out of the court-yard, out of the gateway, out of the road! Let not the field shelter them, nor the garden, nor the grove. Send them to the under-world, let them descend to Illuyankas the dragon.

'Let the heart of Telepinu be comforted; even as the sweet figs that grow on the fig trees, let the heart of Telepinu grow sweet. As the olive holds oil within it, as the grape holds the juice that will become wine, as the dry grain of corn grows up through the ground and the new harvest comes, so be it with the heart of Telepinu. . . .

'Let the sweet and soothing cedar essence lure thee, O Tele-pinu; come home into thy temple, visit once more the Land of Hatti—for in no other land is Telepinu worshipped with sacrifices so pure and with prayers so holy.'

PHOENICIAN

BAAL AND ASHTORETH

EL WAS the Sun-god whom the Phoenicians, who lived in the coast of Syria and Palestine, believed to have created the world, the gods and mankind with the aid of his wife Asherat of the Sea. Although still all-powerful, El grew old; and he decided to hand over the rule of the world to one of his sons.

So he sent for Kothar, the craftsman of the gods, and said to him: 'Make haste, Kothar, and build a palace for Prince Yamm my son, who is also called Nahar the judge, and is the Lord of the Sea. Build a palace of gold and silver; smelt it with fire and let it shine like the sun. Then all will know that Nahar is the great god who shall rule in my place.'

While El was instructing Kothar as to the building of this wonderful palace for Nahar, Ashtoreth the goddess of beauty, on whose forehead shines the evening star, went in haste to seek her brother Baal Hadad, Lord of the Tempests. Sapas the Sun-goddess found him first and to him led Ashtoreth, who said:

'Hearken, great Baal! Our father El has commanded Kothar to build a palace for Nahar more splendid than any that has been seen. Take good heed, for this means that Nahar is to succeed El, and that you will be without honour and without power.'

The great Baal the son of Dagon raged indeed, the lightning flashing from his eyes and the thunder roaring as he cried:

'Nahar shall be driven from the throne of his kingship! My two mighty clubs Ayamur the Driver and Yagrush the Chaser shall break his head!'

Nahar heard this and in haste sent two messengers to El, bidding them say:

'My father El, strong as a bull, give me Baal son of Dagon to be my slave. Let him bow down before me; let all that is his be mine.'

All the gods sat at dinner when the messengers came, and Baal was among them. They bowed their heads and said nothing, but Baal cried: 'Why, oh gods, have you hidden your faces? I see that you are afraid of the messengers of Nahar. Lift up your heads, sit back on your thrones, and hear how I will answer the envoys of Nahar.'

Now the gods sat upright on their thrones while the messengers delivered the words of Nahar without so much as bowing to any but El. When he heard the message from Nahar, El replied:

'Say to my son that I grant his request. Baal shall be his slave for ever. Dagon's son shall be his captive. He shall be sent to him in chains as a gift from the gods.'

Now Baal sprang to his feet in fury, a club in each hand, and would have leapt at the messengers of Nahar, but Ashtoreth held him back, saying:

'Baal, you must not strike envoys. They do but speak the words of Nahar.'

'Then', roared Baal to the messengers, 'go back to your master Nahar and say that I declare war on him! Strong though he is, I will smite him to the earth! However mighty he be, I will grind him to dust!'

When the envoys had gone, Kothar the wise craftsman said: 'Listen to me, Prince Baal, Rider of the Clouds. I tell you that you will smite your enemy, cut him off from life and take his kingdom to be yours for ever more. Go now and smite him with the two clubs I made for you—with Ayamur the Driver and Yagrush the Chaser. Strike him between the shoulders: drive him from his throne!'

Baal needed no encouraging. He rose upon the clouds, his chariot rumbling in the darkness of the storm while his eyes flashed lightning. Nahar stood up against him, but Baal struck him on the head with Ayamur, struck him between the eyes with Yagrush, and Nahar fell to the ground.

Baal leapt upon him to rend him and smash him to pieces, but Ashtoreth stayed his hand, saying:

'For shame, almighty Baal, Rider of the Clouds! Remember who it is who lies before you—no ordinary creature, but Nahar himself, the god of the sea.'

'Baal, I am dying!' said Nahar. 'The kingdom is yours!'

But Nahar did not die, for Baal hearkened to the words of Ashtoreth and did not strike again. Instead he raised Nahar from the ground and sent him with all honour back to his own kingdom of the sea, to rule there for ever and come no more on to dry land to destroy Baal's cities and woods and fields, and the people in them who worshipped him.

In his sea-kingdom, however, Nahar plotted for a while longer to keep Baal from becoming ruler of the Earth. So Baal set out for the palace of Asherat of the waves, the mother goddess from whom all the gods were born, and with him went his sister Anat, goddess of war, and Ashtoreth his queen.

Beneath the waves Baal was welcomed to a great feast by Asherat. At first it seemed that he and Nahar might fall to blows again; but soon it became obvious that Nahar would stand even less chance of victory than before. Asherat had realized already that if Baal did not become the ruler of Heaven and Earth by peaceful means, he would do so by making war against any god who stood in his way. So she not only persuaded Nahar to recognize Baal as his overlord, but promised to do her best to persuade El to accept Baal and have the palace built for him which would prove his position.

So the feast ended happily, and Baal retired to his mountain of Zaphon to wait for the building of his palace.

To bring this about, Asherat of the sea summoned her trusted servant Qadesh the fisherman, and said:

'Saddle a donkey, harness a jackass, put on the harness of silver and the trappings of gold; we must visit El the ancient.'

Qadesh the fisherman did as she commanded, set Asherat on the beautiful back of the jackass and led it towards the pavilion of El, going before her like a shining star.

As soon as El saw her he grinned weakly, twiddled his fingers, and said:

'Why, Lady Asherat of the sea! What are you doing here? Have you become so hungry or so thirsty that your own realm can no longer support you? Welcome to the banquet: eat bread at my table and drain the flagons of wine.'

Asherat sat down to eat and drink with El; and after the meal she said: 'Wise and powerful El, you have done right to make strong Baal ruler over us all and over all the world. One thing only remains to do: send Kothar the craftsman to build a palace for Baal on Zaphon so that gods and men may know his greatness and bow down before him.'

El was so flattered by Asherat's words that he issued his commands at once: 'Go, Kothar, and build a palace for Baal on the heights of Zaphon. Let the mountain supply gold and the hills a treasure of silver so that you may build a house worthy of the great god Baal.'

Hearing these words of El, Anat the goddess of war sped swiftly to bring the good news to Baal, the earth quaking beneath her tread. 'Rejoice, Baal, and receive glad tidings!' she cried. 'El has given his command to Kothar to build you a palace here upon Zaphon more splendid than that of any other god.'

Then Baal rejoiced indeed. He slew an ox and had it ready roasted to set before Kothar the craftsman; and much wine also to

welcome his guest. He said: 'Kothar, build my palace here on Zaphon quickly. Build a great palace in the mountain fastnesses, huge enough to cover a thousand fields—ten thousand acres.'

So the precious cedars were felled on Lebanon and on Sirion; and in seven days the great palace was built on Zaphon and plated with gold and silver so that it shone like fire. Then Baal held in it a great feast to all the gods: bulls and cows without number were slaughtered and roasted; ewe-lambs and he-lambs also; and wine was brought in abundance to make glad their hearts. Then the gods gathered and took joy in the feast, pledging great Baal in flagons of rich wine and acknowledging him to be the greatest of gods and the overlord of them all.

But one god did not come to the feast, nor recognize Baal as master—and that was Mot, who ruled over the dead in the kingdom beneath the earth. Indeed he sent messengers to Baal demanding tribute.

'I alone sway the gods!' cried Baal. 'I will send no tribute to Mot—no, not even from the earth!'

Then war blazed out anew and Anat, Baal's sister the wargoddess, did mighty deeds on his behalf, smiting and smashing in battle on the plain between the two cities of Tyre and Sidon. The slain lay like sheaves of corn, and the hands hung in bundles from her girdle: but every man killed became a subject of Mot's and was no longer a subject of Baal's.

Baal saw what would happen if the war lasted, and he cried to Anat: 'Take away war from the earth! Banish all strife from the soil! Pour peace into the very bosom of the ground!'

So Anat went back to her own palace and there was peace on earth; the ruined cities were rebuilt, the burnt forests began to grow again, and the fresh grass to show above the bare soil.

Mot was still determined to vanquish Baal, and he sent his serpent Lotan, the great leviathan, hugest of all monsters, to fight against him in single combat.

Baal, however, had been taking counsel with gods who were his friends, and in particular with Ashtoreth; and it was she who showed him the only way of overcoming Mot—turning

against him the very means he was using to destroy Baal and his
power.

The serpent Lotan came crawling hungrily up Mount Zaphon
as Baal came out of his palace to meet it. So huge was Lotan that
when he opened his mouth one lip seemed to touch the sky and
the other the earth, while his tongue licked the stars.

The fight was not long, and the end of it was the death of Baal.

'Baal is dead!' cried the messengers who brought the news to
El. 'We found Baal dead upon the ground. Mighty Baal is dead;
the prince, Lord of the Earth, has perished.'

'Baal is dead!' lamented the men and women on earth. 'What
is to become of us now that Baal the son of Dagon has left us?'

The gods mourned too; and Ashtoreth stood weeping by his
body as it was borne to burial on Zaphon. And great was the
sacrifice made in his honour: seventy buffaloes, and the like
number of oxen and cattle, deer and mountain goats and roebucks.

After the mourning for Baal, Anat his sister, the fierce goddess
of war who alone of the living had entry to the land of the dead
(for she herself was Death) stood before the throne of Mot.
'Great Mot, deliver my brother!' she cried. 'Send back Baal
to earth!'

But Mot replied: 'Baal is mine! I have eaten him like a lamb. I
have chewed him in my mouth like a kid. His spirit is my subject
here in my land of the dead, and I will not let him go!'

Then Anat drew her sword and sprang at Mot. She chopped
him into pieces; she burned the pieces with fire; she ground them
in a mill and scattered them on the earth.

Now a wonder was seen. From the earth sprang up corn for the
first time and grew red and ripe for harvest. Then Baal came back
to earth and taught men how to reap the corn and thresh it, how
to grind the grain and make it into bread: and how to sow the
seed for the next harvest.

Mot also regained his power: but henceforth he ruled only the
land of the dead just as Nahar ruled over the sea. For he was now
afraid of Baal, who had conquered death and returned to rule the
earth, and he too made peace with him. Sapas the Sun-goddess

held a feast; and to it came all the gods. Only ancient El and Asherat of the sea were absent; for they were old gods, and the new ones now reigned. All of them paid homage to Baal, and Heaven and Earth were at peace.

So Baal reigned in his shining palace on Mount Zaphon, and Ashtoreth his queen, the lady of love and beauty, dwelt with him. And at last a son was born to bring greater gifts still to the earth— Aleyin, whose part was to cause fresh springs to gush out from the hillside, and the gentle rain to fall on the young crops.

When Aleyin was born Anat brought the news to Baal, crying:

'Receive good tidings, mighty Baal! Rejoice, noble son of Dagon! A son is born to you, Rider of the Clouds! Aleyin is born!'

Baal rejoiced in his palace on Mount Zaphon, and the summer lightning flashed across the sky, while the distant thunder laughed among the mountains.

CRETAN

Zan and Britomartis

THE myths of Egypt and Babylon, of the Hittites and the Phoenicians, are known to us because they were written down by the peoples who believed in them—in Egyptian hieroglyphs, and Babylonian cuneiform, and in the strange alphabets of the Hittites and Phoenicians. But one of the most important of ancient peoples, the Cretans, have left us no written accounts of their gods, no hymns or epics, and indeed no literature at all.

The people of ancient Crete, who are usually called Minoans, after their famous king Minos who comes in so many of the Greek legends, made themselves masters of the sea—the eastern Mediterranean—and lived a peaceful, civilized life on their beautiful island for many hundreds of years. About 1450 B.C. the nearby volcanic island of Thera (Santorin) blew up, and most of the cities of Crete were destroyed by earthquakes and tidal waves caused by this catastrophe. Many of the cities were rebuilt, but the Minoans never quite recovered, and indeed the island was conquered not long afterwards by the Mycenaeans—the ancient Greeks of the legendary period described by Homer and the later poets.

Although the Minoans could write, they had got no further than inventing a clumsy alphabet, with symbols for syllables instead of letters; good enough for making lists and store-orders (many of which have been dug up in Crete and Greece) but no use for writing poems and epics.

Many Minoans seem to have settled in Mycenaean Greece; and they probably had colonies there before the Mycenaeans came. Certainly the Greeks learnt a great deal from the Minoans—including many of their myths and religious beliefs.

But we can hardly ever separate a true Cretan myth from a Greek one. In the Greek myths which follow, the Cretan gods and goddesses are there in the guise of the savage elder gods who are defeated by the younger ones: Cronos and his brothers and sisters who are conquered by Zeus and the rest of the Olympians.

So a good deal of Cretan mythology lurks in the background of Greek myth, and we shall probably never know which story grew out of an old Minoan myth and which is purely Mycenaean.

The Minoans during the Golden Age of Crete, before the explosion of Thera and before the Mycenaeans came, believed in a great mother-goddess whom the Greeks called Rhea.

What the Minoans called her is unknown. Perhaps she was just 'the Mother'; but later she had many names, usually derived from the places specially connected with her. There were no temples to the Great Mother; but there were sacred caves, the most important in Crete being on the mountains of Ida and Dicte, and at Amnisos on the sea coast near Knossos, the great Minoan capital. So she was called Idaea or Dictynna: but one of her names, Hellotis, cannot be explained in this way—so perhaps Hellotis was really the Great Mother's true name.

Hellotis, the Great Mother, wandered through the valleys of Crete and over the wooded mountain sides, and across the great fertile central plain. Where she went the flowers and grass grew, and corn sprang up and ripened into golden grain, while olives and mulberries swelled and darkened on the trees.

At last the time came for her son to be born, and she sought her home in the great cave at Mount Ida. Here the black bees guarded her and gave her honey, while the wild goats brought their milk for the baby Zan.

Lower down the slopes of Ida lived the Dactyls, the five First Men whom Hellotis had made to serve her. Now they made toys to amuse the infant Zan: a rattle of bronze, and little figures out of clay, toys of carved wood and of soft leather and of sheep's wool. Each Dactyl made a toy out of a different material, and these became the models for the crafts of mankind in after days, since Hellotis had made the Dactyls, her 'five fingers', for this very purpose.

When Zan grew older and wandered out of the cave to play on the wooded slopes of Mount Ida, there came out of the forest two bears to look after him. For a whole year Helice the Great Bear guarded Zan, and Cynosura the Little Bear played with him.

At the end of this time Zan was fully grown, and needed a guard no longer. But in memory of his brief childhood on Mount Ida he placed the two bears in the sky among the stars. As for the bees who had protected him when he was a baby, he changed their colour, making them shine like copper with a gleam of gold, and giving them the power to feel no cold, even when the heavy snows fell on Ida in the winter and the cold winds blew keenly round its peak.

For ever after the bees guarded the sacred cave in which lay the toys of the divine child Zan, so that no man could enter it to steal them. Once four wicked Cretans tried to do so. They made bronze armour to cover their heads and bodies so that the bees could not sting them, and walked into the cave. They were just about to lay hands on the sacred toys and steal the honey which the bees stored there, when there came a flash of lightning.

In terror they turned to flee, but as they did so the armour split and fell from them, and the bees rose in a swarm to sting the wicked intruders to death. But then the voice of Zan rang through the place:

'This is the cave of life, and death must not enter it. I spare your lives, evil though you are; but you shall not go back to boast of what you have seen. The only news you shall bring to mankind shall be such messages as I wish to send, which my priests shall translate to the people.'

As Zan spoke the men were changed into birds: into a thrush and a green woodpecker and an owl and another bird whose identity is lost. And ever after the priests of Zan read the omens from the flights of these birds and told the people what was to come.

But meanwhile, after he had grown up on Mount Ida, Zan became the first king of Crete. For the Dactyls married the nymphs of the mountains, whom it seems that Zan or Hellotis made for them by turning the right number of bees into beautiful maidens called Mellisae, 'the Bee-girls'.

Zan too had a wife, the Lady of Ida herself, whose name seems to have been Carme; and they had a daughter called Britomartis, who was a great huntress.

Her gifts to mankind were all concerned with hunting. She taught the use of the bow and arrow, how to chase the wild things with the aid of dogs, and how to catch them in nets. And after

she had invented the net for hunting she showed the people of Knossos how to drag nets through the sea to catch fish.

Britomartis also taught the Cretans to run races; and such sports were held ever after in her honour. But in the end she left Crete for ever, and it was by means of her inventions that she escaped.

While she dwelt in Crete Britomartis seemed an ordinary mortal girl, and Minos the young king of Knossos fell in love with her.

'Beautiful Britomartis, sweet maiden, be my wife!' he begged. 'Great Zan has made me the first king of this land, and has told me that all the kings of Knossos after me shall be called Minos. So be my queen, and our son shall be the next Minos of Crete, and his son and his son's son after him.'

Britomartis, however, would have none of him. 'I do not wish to marry!' she cried. 'My home is on the hillsides and in the deep valleys where the deer are and all the wild creatures of the wood and mountains. Yet, if you can catch me, you shall have me!'

So saying, with a merry laugh Britomartis turned and fled into the forest on the hillside above Knossos, sure of her safety—for none could run as fast as she.

But Minos was deeply in love, and nothing mattered but to win Britomartis. So he left his kingdom and ran after her: up and up into the mountains they went. First up Mount Juktas behind Knossos; and then beyond it to great Ida itself; and so onwards from end to end of Crete.

Minos never managed to come up with Britomartis, but she was never long out of his sight. Once she escaped him only by hiding under a heap of oak leaves, and once by lying in a field of corn; but often it seemed that he would catch her, and she got away only just in time.

Yet she would not give up, nor would he cease from pursuing her; and at length the chase had lasted for nine whole months.

In the end Minos grew desperate. He felt that Britomartis would only be caught if he could corner her somewhere; if there were no escape, she would own herself fairly beaten and become his wife as she had promised.

So he turned her in her flight again and again until at last she fled up Mount Diktaion, which stands on the very edge of the sea. Minos felt his heart beating with triumph, for there was no way back.

On and on went Britomartis until she found herself suddenly on the edge of the high cliff with the deep sea far below her.

'Now I have you!' cried Minos, pausing to regain his breath. 'You are fairly beaten, Britomartis. Yield now, and be my wife, and the queen of beautiful Knossos and all the wide land of Crete!'

'Never!' cried Britomartis. 'Help me now, Father Zan!'

Minos sprang forward with a cry of horror. But it was too late —Britomartis had leapt over the cliff's edge into the sea.

Had she been a mortal maiden Britomartis would certainly have been killed. As it was, however, she landed into the nets which she had taught the fishermen to make; and these saved her from the sharp rocks.

After this Zan took the matter into his own hands and caused the sea to carry her away and away to the island of Aegina, where she was worshipped as the goddess Aphaea, and where her beautiful temple still stands to this day.

Zan himself had left the earth by this time, after teaching mankind to live together in a civilized way with just laws and fair dealings, and to honour the gods and obey the king whom he had appointed to take his place on earth.

When Zan became a god he died as a man and was buried on Mount Juktas near Knossos. In memory of his death a great bull was sacrificed each year; and until the day came it was kept in the city and the young men and maidens played the dangerous Bull Game: vaulting over its back and turning somersaults with their hands holding its horns.

As for the first Minos, to make up for losing Britomartis, Zan gave him Pasiphae the Moon-goddess to be his wife, and the mother of the next king. And ever after there was a Minos to rule over Crete just as there was a Pharaoh to rule over Egypt: each a divine king to take the place of the god—Zan or Osiris—who had ruled over the land as a man at the beginning of time.

GREEK

THE BATTLE FOR OLYMPUS

TRYING to picture to themselves the earliest days of the world, the ancient Greeks imagined strange and awesome monsters—shapes and spirits looming huge and terrible in the distance of time, fighting and struggling together to bring into being the beautiful world, which they saw all round them in Greece and the islands, out of the first shapeless Chaos.

Out of Chaos grew Earth: the world itself and also the spirit of the Earth, the goddess Gaia. Earth came into being with her high mountains such as snow-clad Olympus, and with the dark underworld beneath down as far as the lowest depths of Tartarus.

From Chaos dark Night was born also, and Erebus who filled the empty spaces beneath the Earth. Then Uranus the wide starry Sky came into being, Earth's equal, to be the dwelling-place of the gods.

Earth brought forth the hills and valleys, the springs and the streams, and with them their spirits, the Nymphs who dwelt in them; and the trees grew, each again with its own spirit: Oreads to haunt the mountains and Dryads to dwell in the trees and die when they died, and Naiads to be the spirits of rivers and springs of fresh water.

Uranus and Gaia were also the parents of the Titans, the Old

Gods who reigned before the days of Zeus and the gods of Olympus. Many of these were honoured even when their power passed to the younger gods; and some almost faded into them until the same name might do for either. Oceanus never lost his place as father of the Sea-nymphs who dwelt in the great stream of Ocean which flowed round the whole world, though in time Poseidon became god of the sea; Hyperion and Theia were still held in respect as the spirits of the Sun and Moon, though their children Helios and Selene became the drivers of the chariots of the Sun and Moon; while Themis and Mnemosyne—Law and Order, and Memory—were never cast out of Heaven nor lacked honour in the land of Greece.

Besides these, Uranus and Gaia had three monstrous sons, Briareus, Cottus and Gyes, each with fifty heads and a hundred hands; and three giants, the Cyclopes, who had only one head, but had each a single eye in the middle of his forehead. These monsters Uranus threw down into the darkness under the earth and imprisoned them in Tartarus.

The younger children of Uranus and Gaia were Rhea and Cronos who, among the Old Gods, were accepted as rulers of Earth and Heaven. And indeed Cronos seized the power from his father Uranus with the help of Gaia, who was angry at the imprisonment of so many of her sons in Tartarus.

Gaia gave Cronos a sickle of adamant and told him how he might waylay Uranus, smite him with this sharp weapon and make him harmless.

Cronos did as Gaia instructed him; and when Uranus was powerless and no more to be feared, he made himself ruler of Heaven and married his sister Rhea.

But monstrous Cronos could not reign in peace. Earth warned him that, for his evil deed against his father Uranus, he himself must be cast out of Heaven and imprisoned in Tartarus by one of his own children. So as soon as Rhea bore him a child he swallowed it—first his daughters Hestia and Demeter and Hera, and then his sons Hades and Poseidon.

Rhea was filled with grief at the loss of her children. She tried to hide them, but ogreish Cronos found each in turn, and did not rest until he had swallowed them.

When her youngest child was about to be born, she went in tears to her mother, Gaia, and begged her help. And Gaia promised to tend and protect the child, and advised Rhea how to deceive Cronos.

As soon as Zeus was born on the island of Crete, Gaia took him and hid him in a great cave on Mount Dicte. But Rhea wrapped a stone in baby-clothes and, weeping bitterly, yielded it up to cruel Cronos as his youngest child. And Cronos, thinking that it was indeed the baby Zeus, swallowed the stone and went away well pleased.

'No child of mine shall live!' he cried triumphantly. 'Be it on earth, in Heaven or in the sea, I shall find it—and so no son of mine can grow up to cast me out of Heaven.'

But the baby Zeus was hanging in his cradle at the mouth of the Dictean Cave—and so was indeed neither in Heaven nor on earth nor in the sea. So that Cronos should not hear his cries, Rhea taught a band of young Cretans (called the Curetes) how to dance the sword-dance in honour of Zeus, clashing their weapons again and again on their little round shields. To feed the fast-growing child came the goat Amalthea, and Zeus grew speedily on a diet of goat's milk. He grew so fast that one day in a childish rage he seized Amalthea by one of her horns and broke it off. After this, however, the horn was always filled with ripe fruits and nuts and herbs, which Zeus ate day by day—yet the Horn of Plenty was never empty.

When Zeus was almost fully grown the mountain nymphs brought him such food as a youth needed, and in reward he gave them the Horn of Plenty. But when he became ruler of the heavens he set the goat Amalthea among the stars, renaming her *Capella*.

As soon as he was full grown Zeus made ready for his campaign against Cronos. His very first ally was the nymph Metis, daughter of Oceanus, whose wisdom and prudence were not to be equalled until her daughter Athena was born. Metis told Zeus that his brothers and sisters, whom Cronos had swallowed, must first be freed from their strange prison to help him.

'They are not dead,' Metis told him, 'and indeed they are now fully grown and ready to aid you in your war.'

At first Zeus could think of no way to rescue those who were to be the new gods. But Metis found for him a magic herb which he dropped unseen into the cup of nectar, the wine of Heaven, from which Cronos drank. And the result was that Cronos brought up Poseidon, Hades, Hera, Demeter and Hestia alive and well, and all eager to be revenged on the monster who had swallowed them. Cronos also brought up the stone which he had mistaken for his youngest child, and after the war Zeus set it up at Delphi, the centre of the world—and there it may be seen to this day.

Then Zeus and his brothers and sisters began their war on the Titans; and a few of the children of the Titans sided with them, such as Prometheus and his brother Epimetheus; and some did

not take part in the war, having their duties to perform, such as driving the chariots of the Sun and Moon.

For ten years the war continued, but neither side gained the victory, and for a time there was a lull: Zeus and his followers encamped on Mount Olympus in northern Greece, while Cronos and the Titans occupied Mount Othrys farther south.

During the pause in the war Zeus stole away to Delphi to seek advice from Earth herself, who would sometimes speak from her sacred cave in the foothills of Mount Parnassus over which Apollo's temple was built in later days.

'Earth, Mother Earth, tell me how to defeat the Titans,' begged Zeus. And the deep voice of the oldest prophet of all echoed solemnly up to him in a warm breath of sulphur from below:

'In the earliest days I bore three sons, Briareus, Cottus and Gyes, larger than any that have seen the light of day. Fifty heads has each of them, and a hundred hands—but cruel Uranus was jealous of their strength and cast them down into Tartarus where they are shut up in a flaming prison of brass, guarded by the dragon Campe. Set the hundred-handed free: make them your allies; and you will conquer the Titans and reign supreme over all gods, and over the races of men who will come to dwell on earth when this war is ended.'

Zeus knew that Mother Earth spoke only the truth. So he set out at once for the dreadful land beneath the ground, making his way down and down through the fearful gloom of Erebus until he came to the brazen walls of Tartarus round which flowed Phlegathon, the River of Fire.

In front of the gates of Tartarus crouched the dragon Campe, the most fearful monster ever seen. She had more legs than a caterpillar, but each leg was a writhing serpent spitting poison; and from her neck grew fifty heads of various beasts. Between her neck and her waist she had the body of a gigantic woman, with snakes curling from her arms in place of hairs; and below she was covered with scales like a sea-monster, while her long tail was a scorpion with a sting like a gleaming splinter of sharp ice.

Seeing Zeus this terrible creature rose on her dusky wings and flew roaring to attack him, fire flashing from her many eyes. But Zeus stood his ground, wielding the sickle of adamant with which Cronos had maimed Uranus. Each time she flew at him Zeus cut off one of her heads; and every time she tried to catch him in her snaky legs he mowed them from under her, until at last she fell to the ground and died.

Once Campe was slain the way into Tartarus was clear, and Zeus led out the three Titans and brought them to Mount Olympus, where they were welcomed by the other gods, who set before them the divine food ambrosia, and nectar the wine of Heaven.

After they had been fed and entertained Zeus said to the three Titans:

'Hear me, children of Earth and Heaven: for long we who are the children of Cronos and Rhea have fought against the Titan gods, striving for victory which never comes. Though you are his brothers, you have no more reason to love Cronos than we have; did he set you free from Tartarus into which Uranus had hurled you? On the contrary, he made Campe the dragon to guard its entrance so that you might never again come forth. Then help us now, bearing in mind how I have slain Campe and freed you from Tartarus; and how we, the new gods, have welcomed you to Olympus and given you freely of our nectar and ambrosia.'

Blameless Cottus answered mildly: 'Divine one, all that you say is true and we have thought upon it and considered it in our hearts. You have freed us from Tartarus, which we thought never to leave again; and now we will aid you in your struggle and fight at your side against the Titans. But one thing we advise: deeper still in Tartarus lie bound our brethren the three Cyclopes. Set them at liberty also, and they will forge weapons for our use and yours; for such is their skill.'

Then the heart of Zeus was filled with gladness, and he hastened once more through the deep gloom of Erebus to the brazen walls of Tartarus. There he smote off the bonds which held the mighty Cyclopes, and led them to the caverns under the volcanic island of Lemnos. Here they set up their forge and made weapons and armour for the gods of Olympus: for Poseidon a trident with which to stir up the sea into great storms; for Hades a helmet that made its wearer invisible; and for Zeus himself the mightiest weapon of all—the glowing thunderbolt, and to go with it the blinding flash of lightning and the roar of thunder.

Now once more the gods and goddesses of Olympus made ready for war, Briareus, Cottus and Gyes leading them with great rocks held in their hundred hands. And against them came the army of the Titans, led by the monstrous Cronos and by Atlas the hugest of them all.

Earth and sea were filled with the din; Heaven was shaken and high Olympus reeled on its base until the tremor of earthquake reached even down to distant Tartarus. They hurled their missiles against each other, and the battle cries of each army echoed to the starry sky as they crashed together.

Now Zeus put forth all his power, his heart filled with fury. From high Olympus he came, hurling his lightning; the thunderbolts flew thick and fast from his strong hand while thunder and lightning whirled round him in an awesome flame. The forests crackled loudly with fire and the wide meadows of Thessaly were scorched bare; all the land seethed and the sea boiled and bubbled. The hot vapour and the soaring flames lapped the Titans about and the flashing glare of lightning and thunderbolt blinded their eyes. The heat rose even to Chaos beyond the sky, and it seemed as if Earth and Heaven were crashing together in ruins when the gods and the Titans met in battle.

Through the clouds of smoke and flame, through the dust storms and the earthquakes advanced Cottus, Briareus and Gyes, fighting more fiercely than any. Three hundred rocks, one after another, they launched with their strong hands, and cast down the Titans and seized them and hurled them beneath the earth. For nine nights and nine days the Titans fell through gloomy Erebus under the earth, and on the tenth day landed in Tartarus—there to lie bound for ever.

And there, at the very bottom of the world, the Titans lay in prison, hidden in misty gloom; and over them the great gates were barred, and outside sat Cottus and Gyes and Briareus, always on guard lest the enemies of Zeus should escape.

Only one of the Titans who had fought for Cronos did not lie bound in Tartarus, and this was Atlas, the hugest of them all. Him mighty Zeus set to stand for ever on a high mountain in the north of Africa, holding the sky on his shoulders so that it should never fall upon the earth. And there he stood ever afterwards (though once the great hero Heracles held up the sky for him during a whole night and day), until Zeus in pity let him look upon the head of Medusa the Gorgon, and he was turned to stone and became Mount Atlas.

But the war being won and the reign of Cronos at an end, Zeus and his brothers cast lots for their inheritance. Hades gained dark Erebus, the kingdom under the earth to which the spirits of dead men and women were soon to come as his subjects. Poseidon became lord of the sea, ruler of the waves and shaker of the earth. But Zeus won as his share Heaven and the bright light of day—the kingdom above the earth; and he built his palace in the sky and named it Olympus, after the mountain in northern Greece which he had held against the Titans, which became as it were the earthly mirror of his heavenly home.

In Olympus dwelt Zeus as overlord of all the gods; and in time his children came to dwell there with him. At first he married several wives from among the daughters of the Titans: Metis, the mother of wise Athena; and Dione, who is said to have borne golden Aphrodite, goddess of love and beauty, to him—though she was first seen rising in all her beauty out of the foam of the sea. Later he married Leto, who became the mother of the twins Apollo and Artemis; and Maia, the mother of Hermes the messenger; and later still he married mortal wives, such as Semele, the mother of Dionysus, the god of the vine; and Alcmena, the mother of Heracles, the greatest of the heroes, who became a god after his death as a man.

But in spite of these Zeus made his sister Hera his royal wife and the Queen of Olympus; and their children were Ares the god of war and Hephaestus patron of all craftsmen and smiths; and gentle Hebe who waited upon the gods in Olympus, pouring out the divine nectar at their heavenly feasts.

To these feasts came the Nine Muses, also daughters of Zeus, whose mother was Mnemosyne, the Titan goddess of memory. Their earliest dwelling-place was on Pieria, near Mount Olympus; but later they moved to Helicon in southern Greece, and Apollo the god of music became their leader.

'And it is through the Muses and far-shooting Apollo that there are singers and harpers upon earth, and happy is he whom the Muses love: sweet flows speech from his mouth,' sang Hesiod, one of the earliest poets of Greece. 'For though a man have sorrow and grief in his newly troubled soul, and live in dread because his heart is distressed, yet when a singer, the servant of the Muses, chants the glorious deeds of men of old and the blessed gods who inhabit Olympus, at once he forgets his sadness and remembers not his sorrows at all; for the gifts of these goddesses soon turn him away from all sad thoughts.'

PROMETHEUS THE FIRE-BRINGER

BEFORE the coming of the Olympians, and while Cronos and the Titans still ruled Heaven and earth, there had been one race of men. Theirs was the Golden Age when there was neither sin nor suffering in the world; they lived like gods, without toil or grief, and they never grew old, but spent their lives in dancing and feasting. When they died it was as if they had fallen asleep at the day's ending; and while they lived the earth bore for them all that they needed, and they dwelt in peace, loved by the gods; and in after days their spirits wandered over the earth keeping watch over the men of later times.

The men of the Golden Age had no children, and after them the Titans turned to evil and the great war took place in which Zeus was victorious and set up his rule in his new heaven of Olympus.

When the earth had recovered a little from the fires and earthquakes, the eruptions and the tidal waves which had wrecked it during the war of the Titans, Zeus made another race of men, the Silver Age. But they were less noble than the men of the Golden Age, and lived a life of utter simplicity—a child taking a hundred years to grow up. Yet they lived only a short while when they came to manhood, for they were so foolish that they could not keep from hurting one another and neglecting the gods; and very soon Zeus put them away and made a new race.

But the men of the Bronze Age were no better than those of the Silver Age, though the evil which they did was different. Their only love was for war and deeds of violence; they made armour and weapons and houses of bronze, and were utterly cruel and ate the raw flesh of their enemies. In time they destroyed each other until none were left, and their souls went down to dwell in Erebus, in the darkest part of the kingdom of the dead.

Now the time had come to create a new and a better race of men on earth; and at the beginning of this, the Age of Heroes, Zeus turned for help to one of the old gods, the Titan called Prometheus who had fought on his side during the great war in Heaven. Already the wide earth teemed with life: birds sang in the trees, beasts wandered on the hillsides, and fishes splashed in the waters. But there was no creature more akin to the gods than these. Now Prometheus moulded man out of clay made of the red earth of Panopeus, in the likeness of the gods themselves, and looking up to Heaven as he stood on his two feet—while all animals looked down upon the earth. Then Zeus breathed the breath of life into the first men, and Prometheus dwelt among them as a man himself, with his brother Epimetheus, and taught them all that he felt they should know.

First he taught them to build houses as shelter from the cold of winter and the heat of summer, and how to find food among the fruits and herbs which grew wild, and how to plant and tend them, after clearing away the thorns and briars which grew over the earth. Then he taught them to catch such animals as sheep and goats, and in time cattle, and tame them and use them for food, and their skins and wool for clothing, and their strength to draw the plough and the cart.

Above all he taught men to live according to law and order, to be just and kind to one another, and to worship the gods, pray to them, and offer sacrifices. When they first had the breath of life breathed into them, men could see too much of the future for any true happiness; this power Prometheus took away from them, teaching them to thank the gods for each day as it came and have no dread of what the morrow might bring; and he promised in time to give them the further gift of hope, so that there might be no danger of fear and despair bringing them down once more to the life of savages.

One great gift above all remained unknown to men, and this was fire. Prometheus knew that without it the race of men could never rise any higher: they must have fire to cook their meat, which they still ate raw; to melt copper and tin and forge it into bronze, and later to smelt and shape iron; to bake the pots and cups and bowls which he taught them to make out of clay; and to offer true sacrifices to the gods of incense and the burnt flesh of the sacred animals.

Prometheus knew that Zeus looked doubtfully on what he was doing to raise men towards the gods and further and further from the animals. In this early morning of the world Zeus was still very much of a Titan like his father Cronos; he could be jealous and cruel, and above all he could fear. For there was always the dread lest he should be cast out of Heaven as he had cast Cronos; and he feared lest if men became too powerful even they might make war against him.

Nevertheless Prometheus, though he himself could see far into the future (the one power which Zeus did not possess), had grown to love mankind so much that he decided to offer himself as a sacrifice, if need be, so as to bring the great boon of fire to humans.

At first Zeus seemed likely to grant this supreme gift. Cunningly Prometheus told him how much better men could worship the gods if they had fire, making burnt offerings of the best they had.

On a day Prometheus staked all in the supreme test and invited Zeus to visit the place of sacrifice where he had set up altars, at Sicyon on a hillside near the southern shore of the Gulf of Corinth.

Before Zeus came Prometheus prepared the sacrifice. He killed and cut up a great ox and set the pieces in two piles—one for the sacrifice, and one for his own portion to be the part which men should have ever afterwards when they made offerings to the gods. Now Prometheus knew that Zeus would demand all the best part of any sacrifice; and he knew too that mankind had few oxen and that these were very precious to them. When they killed an ox it would be on some special occasion—they could only afford to eat beef in celebration of some festival, and must feast to the full, and then go back to the small, simple diet of every day.

So he took all the white bones of the ox and covered them cunningly with fat and arranged them most choicely; but the real joints of meat he hid under the offal and the tripe, so that the second pile seemed far inferior to the first.

'Prometheus, most glorious lord, how unfairly you have divided the portions,' said Zeus.

'Greatest of all the immortal gods,' answered Prometheus simply, 'the choice is yours: take whichever portion you will.'

Now Zeus, who knew all things, did not fail to see through the trick which Prometheus was playing him. Although he was not deceived, he chose the portion which was all bones and fat, and let Prometheus win the better half for mankind; and ever afterwards that was the part of the animal which was sacrificed to the gods as a burnt offering, leaving the good meat for the great feast afterwards.

But Zeus still had no real love in his heart for men, as Prometheus had, and he turned angrily to the Titan, saying:

'So you still intend to cheat me, do you, and keep the best for yourself? Since you have taught these humans to pay me such

scant honour, and to think they can trick the deathless gods, I
swear that I will never give them fire!'

Now Prometheus realized that he must steal fire for mankind,
and as a result offer himself as a sacrifice in exchange for it. He
knew that, once it was given, Zeus could not take fire away: but
he knew also how terrible a punishment Zeus would make him
suffer for the theft.

So he made his way to the western verge of the world, where
Helios, who drove the chariot of the Sun, descended into the sea
each night and was ferried in a golden bowl round the stream of
Ocean that encircled the earth to his palace in the east, where Eos
the Dawn-goddess opened the silver doors for him each morning.
Lying in wait near the sea-shore not far from the mountain where
Atlas held up the sky, Prometheus reached up a torch to the wheel
of the Sun-chariot as it passed low over his head, and then trans-
ferred the flame to the pith in the hollow stalk of a giant fennel—
which the Greeks still used for carrying fire within living memory.

Bearing his precious spark in the tall fennel-stalk, Prometheus
hastened across the world until he came back to Greece; and here,
in a wooded valley of Arcadia, he lit the first fire.

As it blazed up brightly in the darkness, the wild creatures
gathered on the edge of the ring of firelight, gazing in awe and
wonder at the mysterious new thing. Among them were the
Satyrs, wild men with horses' tails and little horns growing from
their heads, who were related to the Nymphs, but represented the
thoughts and passions of uncivilized men.

The Satyrs gathered eagerly round the fire, but Prometheus
warned them:

'Do not come too close, lest a sudden gust of wind blows a
flame to burn you: for the breath of fire is hot and scorching.'

But the Satyrs would not be warned, and one of them, in an
ecstasy of delight, exclaimed:

'Let me kiss this wonderful thing!' and burned his beard in
trying to do so.

Then they pranced round the fire, singing: 'How the beautiful
warmth and the kindness of the fire sets us dancing! Throw down

your cloaks and join us! Now we can see the Nymphs and chase them by the light of the fire—and they, we know full well, will join us in dance and song to honour the gift of Prometheus the fire-bringer! Great is Prometheus, who has brought this the

greatest of all gifts to men: let everyone join in dance and song to honour the fire-bringer, great Prometheus!'

But Prometheus knew that he had only a little time, and began at once to teach mankind the many uses of fire—how to cook food, make lamps and warm their houses; how to smelt bronze and gold and silver and iron, and how to use the tools and weapons which they could now make out of bronze to cut wood and stone, to defend themselves against the wolves and lions and bears, and to kill game and cattle for food and to sacrifice by fire to the gods.

He could not escape his fate, however. The time came at last when Zeus looked down from Olympus and saw the sparks of fire scattered about the earth almost as thickly as the stars in Heaven. He knew at once who had done this, and sent for Prometheus.

When the kindly Titan stood before him, Zeus said:

'Son of Iapetus, you who outdo all the world in cunning, you have outwitted me and given fire to mankind. You have disobeyed me and broken the law, so you must suffer the just punishment. As for men, I cannot take away what you have given them, but I will myself make them a gift as the price of fire: an evil thing which will give them great joy as they embrace their own destruction.'

Then Zeus sent Hephaestus with his two strong servants, Force and Might, to bind Prometheus with great chains to the high peak of Mount Caucasus beyond the Black Sea. But he himself set about making Pandora, the First Woman, to bring both pleasure and many woes to mankind.

At his command Hephaestus the god of craftsmen mixed earth with water and made a beautiful shape in the likeness of the goddesses themselves, in seeming like a fair modest maid. And, when Zeus had given her life, Aphrodite shed grace upon her head, but set cruel longings and cares in her heart; then Athena decked her with rich clothes and jewellery, but also taught her the arts of weaving and needlework, while Hermes gave her the power of speech, but put crafty words into her mind and a deceitful nature: and the rest of the immortals gave her other gifts by command of Zeus to bring troubles upon mankind.

When she was complete, Hermes took Pandora down to earth and gave her to Epimetheus, the brother of Prometheus, who was living as a man among men.

Prometheus, fearing what Zeus would do to make men pay for the gift of fire, had warned his brother not to accept any gift from Zeus. But the sight of Pandora was too much for Epimetheus, who was as thoughtless and hotheaded as Prometheus was far-sighted and careful; he fell in love with the First Woman the moment he saw her, and was full of joy when Hermes said:

'Now that Prometheus is no longer here to look after the men whom he has made, Father Zeus has taken them under his care. And he has made the First Woman—whose name is Pandora the "Gifted-by-All", since all the gods gave her gifts at her making— to be your wife. Take her now into your house, and let her rule there as all women shall after her; and she shall tend you, and bring you joy and happiness, and be the mother of your children.'

So Epimetheus and Pandora were married, and in due time their daughter Pyrrha was born, the First Child, and grew up to marry Deucalion, the First Man, whom Prometheus had made, and become the mother of the human race.

But Pandora brought sorrow with her as well as joy. Not only did she tease and trouble Epimetheus, making him jealous and bringing him cares and worries which he had not known before, but she disobeyed him too. For Hermes had brought another gift with him from Olympus and given it secretly to Epimetheus.

'Keep this jar safely,' he said, 'and whatever happens do not open it. It was filled by the gods, your brother Prometheus included, with all the good things which men need and desire. So long as the lid is closed mankind shall enjoy them; but if the lid is raised they will all fly out and return to Heaven.'

Hermes the crafty smiled knowingly as Epimetheus put the jar away in the safest corner of his house; and his smile turned to a broad grin later on when he heard Epimetheus say:

'Now Pandora, my dear, everything that I have is yours. But

one thing only you must not do, and that is to open the jar which I have put away safely in the farthest corner. Be sure that you obey me in this one thing at least.'

Hermes knew well that Pandora, being a woman, would be so filled with curiosity that she would open the jar sooner or later: for he himself had put curiosity in the heart of the First Woman.

And it happened just as Hermes expected and as Zeus had intended. Pandora could think of nothing but the jar, until at last one day when Epimetheus was out she could restrain herself no longer, and took off the lid. Out flew all the countless troubles which plague mankind: every disease that comes by night or day, pain and decay and old age, toil and worry and care. Yet one good thing came to mankind out of the jar—the gift which Prometheus had put there. And this was hope, to help men and women to bear all the ills of this world, hoping ever for happier times and better things to come.

Hope certainly came to Prometheus himself as he lay chained to the peak of Caucasus, suffering in the bitter frosts by night and the burning sun by day. He alone among gods and Titans could look into the future, even though his vision was of what might be rather than of what would be. Even in his exile he was not cut off from the world as the Titans were who lay bound in Tartarus; for the time came when Zeus planned to drown much of the world in a great flood to punish the wicked among mankind who, in the south of Greece at least, had become cannibals. Prometheus knew of this and was able to warn the few men who did not deserve to die to seek refuge with the birds and animals, the Nymphs and Satyrs and the wild Centaurs (half horse, half man) on the mountain tops. In particular he told Deucalion, the First Man whom he had made, and his wife Pyrrha, the daughter of Epimetheus and Pandora, how to build a chest and shut themselves into it until the flood was over. And when after nine days and nights the chest came safely to land on Mount Parnassus, he caused Deucalion and Pyrrha to seek advice from the sacred oracle at Delphi near by as to how they could repeople the land.

'Go forth down the hillside towards the sea,' came the deep

voice from the cleft in the rock where the great Python now guarded the sacred breath of sulphur which carried up the words of the prophecy. 'And as you go, fling behind you the bones of your mother.'

Deucalion and Pyrrha were much puzzled by this; for Deucalion had no mother, and Pyrrha's mother Pandora was lost far away in the great flood.

'I was not born, but made out of the red clay of Panopeus by Prometheus the good Titan,' said Deucalion.

'My mother Pandora was also shaped out of clay by Hephaestus ——' began Pyrrha.

'Then our mother is Earth herself!' cried Deucalion. 'And look! These stones lying on the hillside of Delphi are surely her bones!'

So, as they went, Deucalion and Pyrrha picked up stones and cast them over their shoulders: and, by the will of Zeus, those which he cast turned into men and those which she cast turned into women. And so the earth was repeopled, though the true Greeks believed that they were descended from Deucalion and Pyrrha whose own son, Hellen, gave his name to the Hellenes, the inhabitants of Hellas—the land which is still so called; though the Romans, and we after them, know it as Greece.

Feeling now certain that mankind was safe, and that the race of heroes would not perish, nor their descendants the ordinary men and women of the Iron Age, Prometheus turned his thoughts to his own future and that of Zeus. For a long time he pondered over all that his wise mother Themis had taught him, over all that he could see of the future. Then, when the Sea-nymphs, the daughters of Ocean, came to visit him and weep over his cruel fate, he comforted them, saying:

'I shall not hang here for ever. For even as Cronos fell, so Zeus shall fall and his own son shall cast him down and rule in Heaven and on earth as he now rules. In the future—I will not say how far —there is a bride whom Zeus will plan to wed, and she shall bear a son greater than his father. Then the curse of Cronos will fall on Zeus, and like Cronos his place shall be taken by a new god. . . .

Yet I can save Zeus and prevent this from happening . . . But if I do not, his son will overcome him with a light more fiery than the lightning, an explosive more terrible than the thunderbolt, a weapon against which the bolt of Zeus, the trident of Poseidon, the helmet of Hades will be of no avail.'

Sitting in high Olympus, Zeus saw and heard all. At the words of Prometheus a cold fear struck to his heart, and the terror of the prophecy of his own downfall made him cruel and merciless. In haste he sent his messenger Hermes to distant Caucasus with an offer and a threat:

'Tell Zeus how he may escape the doom which threatens him, and he will release you from your chains. Refuse, and he will torture you until you speak, and then cast you down into Tartarus for ever.'

'I will make no bargains with Zeus,' answered Prometheus, 'and no threat can make me speak against my will, nor any torture which the cruel son of Cronos is able to invent. . . . Yet, at the last, I shall be freed.'

In vain Hermes tried to persuade Prometheus; but all his clever arguments and soft words were of no avail.

'Then hear your fate, and let fear move you!' cried Hermes at last. 'On every second day a great eagle shall swoop down and tear you open. He shall devour your liver, and fly away. Yet you shall not perish, but the liver will grow again and your flesh shall heal—ready for the eagle's next visit. This shall continue until you tell Zeus all that he wishes to know. Moreover, he has sworn that at the last you shall pass to the land of the dead and remain there for ever, unless some other immortal consents to take your place.'

'I knew already of this winged terror who shall torture me,' said Prometheus, 'and I am ready to endure what must be. Yet it can never make me speak.'

So for many hundreds of years Prometheus hung in agony on Caucasus, while the eagle came again and again for its terrible feast, and his cries echoed among the cloud-capped mountains. Ships passing far below at the eastern end of the Black Sea turned and fled away as that terrible cry rang down to them—among them the *Argo* in which Jason and the Argonauts sailed to Colchis in search of the Golden Fleece. High above the ship one evening, as they were turning north up the farthest Black Sea coast towards the mouth of the Phasis on which Colchis stood, they saw the eagle flying near the clouds with a loud whirring sound, making so great a wind with its huge wings that it shook their sails like a storm. And presently they heard the bitter cry of Prometheus, and the air rang with his screams and the mountains echoed them back, until they saw the sated eagle fly slowly away. Then, full of pity and of fear, the Argonauts rowed their hardest and came on the next morning to the mouth of the Phasis which flowed red with the blood of Prometheus.

Yet as the ages passed, Zeus changed. He married many wives, both mortals and immortals, and had many sons; but always the fear was upon him that each son would be the new god who would cast him out of Heaven. Yet still the sons were born and were suffered to live their lives, for there was another prophecy, a warning that Prometheus had given Zeus of a threat to Olympus that would be made by a brood of Giants: 'They can be struck down by the gods,' Prometheus had said, 'but, being the children of Earth, they will leap up again whole and strong as soon as they touch the ground. No immortal can kill them, but a mortal man can do so—the greatest of heroes, who shall be your son.'

And at last that son was born, Heracles the strongest of all men, who passed his life on earth ridding the lands and seas of evil monsters who preyed upon mankind. During his lifetime the Giants came out of their caves in the ground and attacked the gods. Once more Zeus camped upon Mount Olympus, and the Giants piled the nearby mountains of Ossa and Pelion one upon the other to reach the top. The gods routed the Giants and smote them to the ground as they fled across the earth, and Heracles followed and shot each of them with his deadly arrows dipped in the poisonous blood of the Hydra, for which there was no cure in Heaven or upon earth, or in the kingdom beneath the ground.

So this fear was lifted from the heart of Zeus, yet the greater fear remained of the son who would depose him. But the long years of that fear had changed his heart; he had learnt by suffering, and was no longer the cruel tyrant who had bound Prometheus upon Caucasus and sent the eagle to torture him. He determined to free the good Titan from his torture, asking nothing in return, and even before the war with the Giants he sent Heracles to visit him during his quest for the Golden Apples of the Hesperides.

Heracles had no command from Zeus other than to ask Prometheus how to find and win the Golden Apples. He toiled up the steep cliffs of Caucasus until he came to where the Titan lay chained against the rocky peak. As he drew near the eagle swooped suddenly down to its dreadful feast. With a cry of pity and anger Heracles fitted an arrow to his mighty bow and sent it through the eagle's heart. The huge bird towered up into the sky and fell dead into the Black Sea far below, while Zeus caught the arrow and set it among the stars as the constellation *Sagitta*.

Then Heracles turned and struck the metal bands and fetters from the Titan's arms and legs, and Prometheus rose slowly and greeted his liberator.

'You are Heracles, the son of Zeus who was my enemy,' he said. 'I knew that you could come, though I did not know how the heart of Zeus would change. . . . His heart may change, but what he has sworn cannot be changed. Therefore you must be bound by metal bands in my place, and so must all the race of men for whom I suffered. From now on they shall wear rings of metal on their fingers—of gold or silver, iron or bronze or copper—in memory of my bondage. . . . Now I must go through the world seeking if I may find any immortal who will take my place when the time comes for me to go down into Erebus, the kingdom of the dead where Hades rules; for Zeus has sworn to send me thither unless some immortal will go there to take my place, and his oath must not be broken.'

'Then seek out the Centaur called Cheiron,' said Heracles. 'He dwells in a cave on Mount Pelion in Greece, and is the best and wisest of all the Centaurs. Among them he alone is immortal, for his father was Cronos himself. He is famous throughout the land for his skill in hunting, medicine, music and gymnastics, and many of the heroes of Greece go to him when they are young and dwell for a while with him to learn all that a hero should know. Jason the Argonaut was among his pupils, and at present a young man called Peleus dwells with him. Cheiron is my friend, and he would have saved me from the other Centaurs, who are both wild and mortal, who attacked me when they were maddened by wine. By a cruel mischance during the battle one of my poisoned arrows passed right through a Centaur who sought my life, and wounded Cheiron. Neither mortal nor immortal can cure that wound, since my arrow was dipped in the poisonous blood of the Hydra, and now Cheiron is in constant pain and prays for the death which cannot be his, as he is an immortal.'

It seems that Prometheus followed the advice of Heracles and went to find the wise Centaur Cheiron, who agreed to take his place among the dead where the body suffers no more—except in the case of those who are punished in Tartarus for very grievous sins. But the exchange did not take place at once, since Cheiron knew, or perhaps learned from Prometheus, that there would be one more generation of heroes before the Heroic Age ended, and that he was still needed on earth to be the tutor of such men as Diomedes and Achilles.

For Zeus was now planning the great war of Troy, after which the Heroic Age would end and the gods mingle no more with mortal men and women, and marry no more human wives. To bring the war about, Zeus became the father of the most beautiful of all mortal women, Helen of Troy; and he decided to marry the Sea-nymph Thetis and be by her the father of a great hero who would lead the Greeks against Troy and do deeds that would be remembered for ever.

As soon as Prometheus knew what Zeus intended, he made his way to Olympus and stood before the son of Cronos who had been his enemy. Now neither spoke of their ancient quarrel, nor held any thought of revenge in their hearts against each other. But Prometheus the wise spoke, saying:

'Zeus, you who are now indeed worthy to be called the father of gods and men, I warned you once of what fate held in store for you—that as Cronos fell you would fall also, overthrown by a son of yours even as you overthrew your father. Only I could tell you how to avoid this fate, and neither bribes, nor force, nor cruelty could make me speak. But now that you have put away cruelty and set me free, asking no reward for doing so, I will tell you what I would not tell before. There is a prophecy uttered by wise Themis in the days when Cronos ruled, and I alone know it:

"'The son of Thetis shall be greater than his father.' That is all; yet if you wed Thetis, it is enough to cast you from your throne as you cast Cronos, and bring in a new dynasty of the gods.'

Then Zeus was filled with gladness, and welcomed Prometheus back to heaven, bidding him take his place in Olympus once more, or go freely up and down the earth as he pleased, doing all that he could to help the kindly race of men.

On the advice of Prometheus Zeus chose the hero Peleus to be the husband of Thetis; and when he had won her with Cheiron's help a great wedding feast was held in the Centaur's cave on Mount Pelion. To it came all the gods and goddesses of Olympus, and Prometheus among them. At that wedding only Eris, the goddess of strife, was forgotten; and she came uninvited and cast on the board the Golden Apple inscribed 'For the Fairest', over which Hera, Aphrodite and Athena quarrelled until, at the command of Zeus, Paris of Troy was made the judge, chose Aphrodite, and so brought about the Trojan War.

The greatest and most famous hero who fought in that war was Achilles, the son of Thetis and Peleus, who was the last pupil to be trained by Cheiron. For when Achilles left him the wise Centaur knew that his task on earth was accomplished, and he could seek rest in the world of the dead, and with it an end of the unceasing pain of the wound made by the arrow dipped in the Hydra's blood.

So, by permission of Zeus, Cheiron took upon himself the fate of Prometheus that, though an immortal, he must pass down into dark Erebus and dwell as a dead man among the dead.

DEMETER AND PERSEPHONE

IN THE dark land of Erebus, under the earth, Hades was king.
There he sat in lonely state, ruling over the souls of the dead
who came to his realm of shadows across the black waters of
the River Styx as soon as Death had touched them with his sword,
and the flames of the funeral pyre had released them from their
bodies in the world above.

Hades had won his realm after the defeat of the Titans, when
he and his brothers Zeus and Poseidon cast lots for their kingdoms, Zeus winning the sky and Poseidon the sea. Their three

sisters had also a share in the new order: Hera became queen of Heaven as the wife of Zeus, gentle Hestia received the first honour in every human household as goddess of the Sacred Hearth, the centre of family life when fire, the gift of Prometheus, was so hard to come by that it must never be allowed to die; and Demeter ruled over the plants of the earth, and in particular the corn, on which the life of man depended.

Hades was not satisfied, however, with his dark and lonely existence, and he begged Zeus to give him the Flower Maiden, Persephone, the daughter of Demeter, to be his bride. Zeus knew that Demeter would never give her consent, so he told Hades that he must carry off the maiden secretly when her mother was far away.

His moment came when Persephone was gathering flowers with the daughters of Ocean on the fair field of Enna in Sicily—roses and crocuses, and beautiful violets, irises and hyacinths. As she wandered among the flowers, as bright as the very spring, with the sun shining on her golden hair, singing as gaily as the birds themselves, Persephone saw a new blossom the wonder of which lured her away from her companions. It was a thing of awe, this new flower, a wonder that either the deathless gods or mortal men might well stop to marvel at. From its root grew a hundred blooms, and its scent was so sweet that earth and the swelling sea seemed to laugh with the joy of it.

Persephone stooped to pluck the flower of death; but as she reached out her white hands towards it, the earth split open and through the yawning chasm came Hades, the Lord of Many Guests, in his dark chariot drawn by great black horses.

Swift as death the Dark King seized the shining maiden and carried her away so quickly that none saw her go, save only Hecate the Queen Witch as she sat in her cave on Mount Etna. Helios, driving his chariot of the Sun across the sky, saw also, but he could not turn away from his course until the day was done.

Meanwhile, as the Sea-nymphs, the daughters of Ocean, searched this way and that in vain for their lost companion, Hades was sweeping across land and sea in his dark chariot bearing his unwilling bride.

So long as Persephone could still see the green earth and the sky she continued to cry out for help, hoping that her mother Demeter would hear; or that Zeus himself might come to her aid. They came to the land of Greece and sped across the great mountains of Arcadia, towards Argolis, and her heart leapt with joy: for there in her mountain cave looking across to Phigalia dwelt Demeter. Then Persephone gave her last great cry for help as Hades swooped down across the Maiden Mountain, Parthenia, over the blue Gulf of Argolis and into the great chasm by Hermione which leads straight to the land of the dead.

When men died and went to the realm of Hades a coin, the obol, was placed under their tongues in ancient Greece to pay the ferryman, Charon, for their passage across Styx. But the people of Hermione sent their dead to Erebus without a fee, having the back door of the Underworld placed so conveniently for their use.

From where she sat in her cave above Lycosura, Demeter heard Persephone's last despairing cry echoing among the mountains and ringing across the sea. Then bitter pain seized her heart, and she gathered her dark cloak about her and sped hither and thither over land and sea seeking her lost child. But no one knew where Persephone had gone; or no one among gods or mortals or the birds who see all things dared to tell the sorrowing goddess.

For nine days Demeter travelled hither and thither, and as she wandered on the slopes of Etna on the ninth night when no moon shone, Hecate met her, carrying torches in her hands, and said:

'Queenly Demeter, bringer of seasons and giver of good gifts, indeed I know not who has stolen your daughter the maiden Persephone as she played in these fields of Enna. But stolen she was, for I heard her cry as I sat in my cave, and looking out I saw a black chariot speeding away into the distance.'

Thanking her, Demeter took torches in her own hands, lit them in the fires of Etna, and continued her search through the night as well as through the day.

Still, however, she could not find Persephone; and at last she went to Helios himself, waiting to speak with him as he drove the chariot of the Sun down into the western ocean to be ferried round to the east before the morning.

Helios, the watchman of both gods and men, was standing at his horses' heads when Demeter came to him and said:

'Helios, if ever by word or deed I have cheered your heart, help me now. You who look down day by day over land and sea, tell me truly if you have seen who carried away my lovely daughter against her will. For I heard her cry ringing on the empty air, and she was gone before I could come to her from my cave in Arcadia, and I can find no trace of her.'

Then shining Helios answered: 'Queen Demeter, stately daughter of rich-haired Rhea, I will tell you all the truth. None but Zeus himself is to blame, for he gave your lovely daughter Persephone to be the bride of Hades his brother. And Hades seized her as she strayed from her companions on the rich slopes of Etna, and carried her in spite of her cries down through the ground at Hermione to Erebus, his own realm of mist and gloom. Yet, goddess, cease from your wanderings and your loud lamentations: Hades, the ruler of many, is no unfit husband for your child, and she will be his queen and reign with him over the third part of the world which was his share when Cronos fell.'

Demeter answered nothing, but her anger blazed up more fiercely than before, and her rage against Zeus was so great that she went no longer to the heavenly halls of Olympus, but disguised herself as a mortal woman and wandered over the earth.

Unknown to gods and men, she came at last to Eleusis in the land of Attica, not far from Athens, and sat sorrowfully down by the Well of Fair Dances where the women came to draw water. The well is there to this day, and the rock beside it, on which Demeter sat in the shade of an olive tree, has ever since been called *Agelastos*—'the Stone of No Laughter'.

There the four young daughters of Celeus, King of Eleusis, found her when they came with their pitchers of bronze, and asked her who she was and why she sat sorrowing there.

Then Demeter made answer with a feigned tale: 'Greetings,

dear children, whoever your fortunate parents may be. My story is simple: I am called Doso, and my home is in the island of Crete. I came here against my will, for pirates captured me and I only escaped when they put into the harbour of Thoricos beyond Athens. And now I have wandered for many days over hills and by the shore of the sea, and do not know where I am. I can go no farther; but take pity on me, dear children, and give me such tasks to perform as suits a woman of my age.'

The four maidens welcomed Demeter kindly, and led her to their father's palace, where they took her to their mother, Queen Metaneira, who sat on her couch by a pillar holding her baby son Demophon, her youngest born.

Metaneira rose from her place, greeted Demeter kindly, and bade her be seated. But Demeter would not sit, until at length Iambe the serving maid set a stool for her and flung a fleecy sheepskin over it. There she sat, her face covered by her veil, refusing to be comforted until once again Iambe came to the rescue, and brought a smile to the lips of the goddess and a laugh to ease her sorrow by her rough and homely jests and stories.

Yet still she would touch no food, nor drink of the sweet wine which was offered her. But at length she bade them mix meal and water into a thin broth, and flavour it with mint, and she drank of this, which was ever afterwards called *Kykeon*—'the sacred cup of Demeter'.

Then said Metaneira the queen: 'Lady—for I am sure that you are nobly born, since truly dignity and grace look from your eyes —since you have come here wishing to serve me, you shall have all that I can bestow. But for it, I beg of you to nurse my little son Demophon, the child of my old age, who is still a baby in arms; and also to have a care for my other son, Triptolemus, who is yet no more than a child.'

'Gladly will I take the babe and nurse him,' answered Demeter, 'and the boy Triptolemus also shall be my charge. For my own child is lost, and my heart cries out towards those for whom I may care.'

Then she took Demophon in her arms and began to tend him.

And as the days went by he grew so fast and so strangely that Metaneira in her foolish curiosity lay hid one night to see what the strange nurse did to the child.

When all the house was still, Demeter rose and took the baby Demophon. Stripping off his clothes, she anointed him with ambrosia, the sweet food of the gods, and placed him in the heart of the fire, where he lay quite unharmed, laughing happily and snatching at the flames all round him.

But when Metaneira saw what was happening she rushed forward shrieking:

'Demophon, my son! This wicked stranger would burn you to ashes in the fire!'

Even as she cried the baby gave a sudden scream, and a moment later he was indeed no more than a heap of ashes.

Demeter turned towards the foolish queen, her disguise falling from her in her wrath so that she shone forth in all the majestic glory of a goddess, and cried:

'Witless and unbelieving mortal, see what you have done! In your heedlessness and idle curiosity you have marred your fortunes and killed your child. For I would have made him ageless and deathless even as are the blessed gods, and unfailing honour would have been his and yours. For know that I am Demeter, equal to any of the immortal gods, and the cause of joy to gods and to mortal men.'

Metaneira knelt before her, begging for forgiveness and pity; and as her wrath died away Demeter said:

'I cannot undo the evil that you have wrought. But I will bring what honour I can to your other son Triptolemus. When he is of age he shall go forth over the earth in my dragon-car teaching all men how to sow the rich grain in the dark soil so that corn may grow; how to tend it and reap it, how to thresh out the golden grain and grind it into flour. . . . But this cannot be while my daughter Persephone is lost to me. Therefore I command you to build me a temple here in Eleusis, and in it I shall sit in my sorrow until Zeus, father of gods and men, restores to me my lost Persephone.'

All things were done as Demeter commanded. King Celeus gathered together the people of Eleusis, and they built a temple on the hillside in which the goddess sat and lamented for her daughter.

She stayed there for a year, nor once visited Olympus; and a cruel year it was for mankind throughout the world. For no green thing grew out of the earth; in vain the oxen laboured at the yoke, dragging the curved plough through the soil; in vain was the seed scattered in the furrows.

Then a great famine came upon the world, and the race of men would have perished utterly had not Zeus taken note of all that was happening and sent golden-winged Iris, who brings the summer showers, down from Heaven by the bright path of the rainbow to visit Demeter.

'Noble goddess,' she said, 'Father Zeus sends me to bid you come back to Olympus and spread your bounty once more over the wide earth.'

But Demeter paid no attention to her words; nor could any of the gods move her, though Zeus sent each in turn with persuasive bribes and promises. Still she sat alone at Eleusis, stubbornly rejecting all their words, vowing that she would never again set foot on Olympus nor let any green thing grow out of the ground until Persephone was restored to her.

At last Zeus sent his son, the messenger Hermes who leads the souls of the dead on their last journey down to the realm of Hades. Down to that dark kingdom went Hermes of the golden wand, and found grim Hades seated on his throne with his pale bride beside him, her eyes heavy with sorrow as she yearned for her mother and the bright fields of upper earth.

Then said Hermes, bowing low before the king of the dead:

'Dark-haired Hades, mighty ruler over the shades of the departed, Father Zeus bids me lead sweet Persephone back into the upper world and bring her before the blessed gods so that Demeter her mother may see her once more and cease from her sorrow and her anger. For if you do not let Persephone go, Demeter plans to blot out the whole race of men by keeping the seeds of all green things from growing out of the earth. And if this comes to pass, Zeus will have none to rule in the world above, nor will subjects come to your kingdom after a little while.'

'Go, my fair queen,' said Hades of the grim smile, leading Persephone down from the throne and setting her hand in that of Hermes the guide. 'Go, since Zeus commands it; but feel kindly in your heart towards me, who am well worthy to be your husband. And remember that while you are in my realm you rule all who dwell here. Moreover, in the world above it shall go hard with any who do not honour you; for I have but to send my servant Death to touch them on the shoulder, and at once they will become your subjects for ever more.'

Then he called for his chariot and black horses and, giving Hermes the reins, mounted with Persephone beside him, and cleft a pathway through the earth. Up they went, and came to Eleusis where Demeter still sat sorrowing in her temple.

When she saw her daughter Demeter rushed forth and caught her in her arms with a cry of joy. Yet a moment later she paused, struck by a sudden doubt.

'My child,' she cried, 'tell me quickly! Have you come back to me indeed, or must you return to the dark land where Hades rules? Tell me—when you dwelt there did you taste food? For if you did then you cannot escape from the world of the dead.'

In her eagerness to escape for ever from the dark kingdom Persephone swore that she had touched no food since being carried away from Enna. Slow-smiling Hades, however, declared that she had eaten the seeds of a sweet pomegranate which he had given her.

While the matter was in doubt, there came up out of the passage to the underworld a certain Ascalaphus, son of sad Acheron, the second river of the dead, and bore witness against Persephone, saying:

'I saw the queen, the bride of my lord Hades, eating the seeds of the pomegranate in the shadowy orchard of her kingdom and his. And I swear by black Styx, the oath that may not be broken, that my testimony is true.'

Then Demeter knew that it must be so, and in her fury she caused Ascalaphus to be imprisoned under a rock in the realm of Hades as a lesson to all informers. There he lay until the great hero Heracles came to carry away Cerberus, the three-headed dog who keeps watch lest any should escape. Heracles took pity on him and rolled away the rock, and Demeter then changed Ascalaphus into an owl, the bird of ill omen who flits through the darkness screeching of sorrows to come.

Meanwhile Persephone confessed that she had indeed eaten the pomegranate seeds, not fearing any harm, and their joy might have been turned to grief had not Zeus decided that she should divide her time between the two worlds.

So for a third part of every year Persephone dwelt with her husband Hades as queen of the dead; and there her daughters were born, the Furies who bring vengeance on murderers, who in time became the Eumenides, the 'Kindly Ones', guarding the sacred ties of family life and the duty of children to parents.

When Persephone dwelt with Hades, Demeter put on mourning once more and the whole earth mourned with her, bringing cold winter to mankind.

But when Persephone returned out of the darkness the spring came with her and the whole earth put on the green of the grass and leaves and a gay wealth of flowers, while the young corn pushed up through the ground to grow in summer until the fields were as golden with grain as the golden hair of lovely Persephone herself.

Yet the gold faded each year and winter came again as Persephone returned to the land of the dead. But each year she left behind her the promise and the hope of the new life when spring came round once more. The sacred mysteries which the Greeks celebrated at Eleusis showed in the form of a mystery play or ceremony the story of Persephone and her message of comfort and hope—that death is not the end of all, but that there is a new life to follow for those who are pure of heart.

APOLLO THE DRAGON-SLAYER

HERA, the queen of Heaven, was the goddess of marriage
and of the home. As such she was naturally jealous when
Zeus left her from time to time to marry mortal wives.
But she was more jealous when his lady-love was an immortal, a
nymph or the daughter of a Titan, and most jealous when he
married Leto, daughter of Phoebe who had been the Moon-
goddess during the reign of the Titans. For Zeus told the immortals of Olympus that the son whom Leto would bear was Apollo,
the most beautiful of all the gods.

'I am also the goddess of childbirth!' cried Hera defiantly. 'And I shall see to it that Leto bears no child anywhere beneath the ground, nor anywhere on earth where the sun shines by day or the moon and stars by night!'

Then she set her son Ares, the war lord, to watch on top of a mountain in northern Greece, and Iris her messenger whose path is by the rainbow bridge, to look out from another mountain in Asia Minor.

Now Leto was dwelling at beautiful Delphi, in central Greece, where the oracle of Earth spoke in the sulphur vapour that came up through a cleft in the rock on the hillside below the cliffs of Parnassus. For there Zeus had decreed that Apollo was to have his most holy shrine and his most beautiful temple.

When Ares and Iris saw where Leto was they told Hera; and the jealous goddess sent the great she-dragon Python up out of the cleft in the rock to slay Leto. She fled in terror; but Python would certainly have caught her had not Zeus been watching too, and sent Kaikias the North-west Wind to carry her away in his chariot.

Far and far over the sea and land went Leto, always pursued by Python the dragon. From city to city and land to land she went; but none of them would receive her, nor let her pause in her flight: for all feared the terrible Python and the anger of jealous Hera. Weary and sad, Leto wandered on over the sea in the windy chariot of Kaikias, seeking in vain for an island that would let her rest on it. But the Nymph of each island to which she came shook her head sadly, and cried:

'Poor Leto, fly still farther! Here you cannot rest, for fear of the wrath of Hera, and of the dragon Python, who would surely send my poor island to the bottom of the sea if I received you upon it.'

At last Leto's shining sister Asteria the Star Maiden went to Olympus to beg help from Zeus. And he whispered to her how, with the aid of Poseidon, Lord of the Sea, and her own power of shape-shifting, Asteria might deceive Hera and make a resting-place for Leto.

Away sped Asteria, taking the shape of a quail to avoid notice and travel more swiftly over the sea. When dark night came she turned herself into an island—Ortygia the Quail-island—which floated on the sea, guided by Poseidon himself.

Leto, almost at her wits' end, had just reached the island of Rheneia near Myconos. As usual the Nymph of Rheneia shook her head sadly and bade Leto leave her shores: for Python was not far behind her, and Ares and Iris were still on watch to tell Hera if any island gave shelter to her rival.

As Leto stood on the stony shore of Rheneia waiting for the wind chariot to bear her on over the sea once more, she suddenly saw a new island floating towards her. As it touched the shore she stepped on to it; and at once it floated away and came to rest less than a mile from Rheneia; for as it paused Zeus sent great chains of adamant to anchor it in place.

Now Asteria came to her as the Nymph of the island of Ortygia; and Leto knew that she had found a resting-place at last.

Asteria led her to a palm tree beside a little round lake fed by a stream from the island's one hill; and there Leto sank down to rest.

'My island is not on earth, nor yet under it,' said Asteria.

'But the sun will shine on it in the morning,' sighed Leto doubtfully, 'even as the stars shine above it tonight. And when it is day, Ares or Iris will see that you have given me a resting-place.'

'Poseidon, Lord of the Sea, will attend to that before the morning,' answered Asteria; 'and as for now: I am the Lady of the Stars, and they will tell no tales. Nor will Selene the Moon-goddess drive her silver car across the sky tonight; for my daughter Hecate the Queen Witch reigns between the waning and the waxing of the moon, on such a night as this when no moon shines.'

So Leto leaned back happily against the palm tree; and on that night, during the dark of the moon, Poseidon raised such a storm that the sea arched in a great curved wave over the island of Ortygia, so that when the sun rose it was hidden from his sight and from the sight of Hera and her watchers. Yet not a drop of salt water fell on the island while Leto bore her son Apollo and his twin sister Artemis.

For four days and nights the storm raged and the great dome of water covered the dark island of Ortygia. Yet during those days strange things happened there. First of all, wise Themis, the thoughtful Titaness who was the mother of Prometheus, came to visit her niece Leto, bringing with her ambrosia and nectar, the divine food and wine of the gods. Nourished on these, Apollo and Artemis were fully grown by the fourth day. Then Hephaestus, the smith of the gods, came to them bringing to each, by command of Zeus, a golden bow and a quiver full of arrows.

At once the waves drew back and a great calm fell on the sea. The dark island, which until then had been called Ortygia, shone out like a star on the breast of the ocean, and by the will of Zeus received the name of Delos. In honour of the Star Maiden Asteria it shone, and shines still, more brightly than any other island, for its stones and rocks are filled with shimmering specks of mica which catch and reflect the sun. But afterwards, in honour of Apollo and Artemis, shrines and temples were built all round the sacred lake, and a temple of glittering stone and marble on the hill of Cynthus: and no sailor sighted the shining temple of Apollo without turning aside to do him and his sister honour in holy Delos.

Meanwhile Artemis and Apollo stood together on the island when the great wave drew back, and fitted each an arrow to their golden bows. But the dragon Python saw them, and did not think any more about following Leto. Instead she turned tail and sped back to Delphi, where she hid in another and a deeper cave under the shadow of Parnassus, where a beautiful clear stream of water gushed out from the Castilian Fountain.

Artemis laughed merrily. 'My first day's hunting has brought me little gain!' she cried. 'Now I will seek the deep valleys and the wooded hills of Arcadia, and gather nymphs about me to be my companions of the chase. I will never marry, for all my days shall be spent in hunting, and my nights too under the bright moon. But my golden arrows shall also bring swift and invisible death to the wives and daughters of men, when Father Zeus so commands.'

'My golden arrows shall deal death to men when Zeus bids me send swift pestilence among them,' answered Apollo; 'but I will also teach how to cure sickness and heal wounds—until the time comes when my son Asklepios is raised to Heaven and becomes the god of healing. One day—and I have not long to wait—I shall be the lord of music and lead the Muses as I play on my sweet-toned lyre, which is not yet known to gods or men. But now I will go through the land of Greece to find a place where my holy Oracle shall be, and my priestess shall speak my will and tell of things to come when men bring gifts and do honour to me at my shrine.'

So Apollo passed over the sea to Greece and wandered to Dodona where the Oracle of Zeus whispered through the leaves of the great oak trees in the sacred grove. There Zeus told him that he was indeed to have an oracle which would become the most famous in the whole world, and the truest; but that he must find the place appointed for it, where until he made it his own great Earth herself had spoken words of truth, and that the place would be called Delphi.

Apollo left Dodona and made his way southwards through Greece—by Oechalia and Trachis, and so eastwards to Thebes and the plain by Lake Copais to a fair river flowing from a mountain gorge, and decided that this was the place for his temple. He had just marked out the foundations, and engaged two young men called Agamedes and Trophonius to build the temple, when Telphusa, the Nymph of the River, rose out of the water and said to him:

'Lord Apollo, I have a word of counsel for you. Do not build your temple here, for it is beside the road leading from Thebes through the mountains to the sea. Many will pass by in brazen chariots drawn by horses and with mules pulling carts, and the noise will disturb you. Moreover the men who should be tending to your temple and the rites of your shrine will neglect their duties and stand gazing at the shining chariots and the swift-footed horses. My advice is that you follow the road until it passes down the valley leaving high Parnassus on your right; there on the hillside beneath the cliff is a place called Crisa, which is so beautiful that it is more worthy than any other to be the site of your holy shrine. Up there, by the cleft in the rock, you will be so far from the road in the valley that there will be no clashing of bright chariots nor noise of swift-footed horses to stir the peace of your sacred enclosure.'

So spoke Telphusa. Yet, though her words were sweet, her heart was filled with anger that Apollo should wish to build near her fountain and so take away from the honour that was paid to her. Moreover, she knew who dwelt in the cleft of the rock near Crisa—which was not yet named Delphi.

Suspecting no evil, Apollo thanked the nymph and continued

on his way through the passes of the mountains until he came to where the River Pleistos flowed steeply down a deep valley with tall Parnassus rearing cliffs of golden yellow rock on one side. He came to Crisa, which is now called Delphi, and found the place where Mother Earth spoke through the breath of sulphur from below. And indeed it was the most beautiful place in the whole world, with the great mountain behind it, and below the deep green valley leading down to the tree-covered plain beyond which gleamed the blue sea-water of the Gulf of Corinth.

Here once more he drew out the plan of his temple, setting one end above the place where the sulphur breath of Earth rose up from the cleft in the rock. And soon Agamedes and Trophonius were labouring hard, levelling the ground, smoothing and setting the stones to make the platform, and felling straight, thick trees for the pillars of the temple, until the day should come when fluted drums of stone and marble should take their place; and, instead of painted wood, beautifully carved marble pediments and friezes, tinted in many rich hues and tricked out with gold, should make of Delphi a shrine fit for shining Apollo.

When a beginning had been made of the building of his temple, Apollo turned his steps to the narrow gorge in the rocks through which the clear cold water of the Castalian Fountain flowed out of the cave beneath Parnassus and down to join the River Pleistos in the valley below.

'I am minded', mused Apollo, 'to make of Castalia the sacred spring of poesy and song at which minstrels and poets through the ages shall drink in my honour and receive inspiration from me and from the Nine Muses—though they shall also find honour on Mount Helicon where the Fountain of Hippocrene blushes pink in the dawn——'

Apollo paused suddenly in his thoughts and strung his golden bow in haste. For from the Gorge of Castalia came a hissing sound, and out rushed the she-dragon, Python, who had hidden there when Leto escaped her. Now she came out only by night to do great mischief to men and beasts; but seeing Apollo she thought to slay him speedily, deeming that he was unarmed.

But swift as light, even as the dragoness charged with open mouth, Apollo fitted an arrow to his bow, drew, loosed and sprang aside. Then Python, mortally wounded, rolled over down the hillside, Apollo following and shooting arrow after arrow until at last the monster lay dead.

'Now rot there upon the soil!' Apollo cried in triumph. 'You shall no longer be a plague to either gods or men, nor shall mankind ever again fear to draw nigh my sacred oracle, bringing rich offerings of gold.'

But Earth cried out for justice at the death of her child, and Zeus commanded Apollo to do penance for his deed, even though he had rid the land of an evil menace and slain only in self-defence.

'You shall go a pilgrim on foot to the beautiful Vale of Tempe,' he commanded, 'and there be purified for your sin. Moreover, though the oracle here at Delphi is now yours, in memory of this child of Earth who guarded it for her in the ancient days, the oracle shall be called Pytho, and the great games to be celebrated here in your honour shall be dedicated to you as the Pythian Apollo.'

Bowing to the will of Zeus, Apollo twined a wreath of ivy round his head and set out on the long journey to the north of Greece, leaving Delphi by the path which afterwards became the Sacred Way. He came at length by the plain of Thessaly to where the Vale of Tempe lies between the mountains of Olympus and Ossa, the beautiful River Peneus passing through it on its way to the sea, and helping to make of it a plot of land so lovely that the Greeks wrote of it as the earthly Paradise. There were tall oak trees growing on either slope, and thick yews, and many other trees; the birds sang more sweetly than anywhere else as they flew from grove to shady grove, or perched among the green leaves and blossoms. The rocks were clad with ivy, and the clearings by the river side were rich gardens growing without the aid of man, nor did anyone who lived there need to till the soil.

Apollo made his sacrifice and received his purification on an altar to which the young men of Delphi ever afterwards made a pilgrimage at eight-yearly intervals in memory of his visit.

As he turned to begin his journey back to Delphi, the beautiful nymph Daphne, daughter of the River Peneus, stepped out of the wood, and Apollo saw her and loved her at sight.

Seeing the shining stranger, Daphne was seized with sudden panic, and she turned and fled without waiting to hear his words:

'Stay, lovely nymph!' cried Apollo. 'You shall be my bride. And the wife of Apollo of the golden bow will have no less honour than the goddesses themselves who dwell in the halls of the heavenly Olympus.'

But Daphne would not listen, and she sped away with Apollo after her, running in her panic away from the River Peneus where she would have been safe. On the steep slope of Ossa Apollo overtook her fast, though by the time he came up with her he had no breath left for words, but could only clasp her in his arms.

But she could just gasp: 'Save me, Mother Earth! Turn me into what you will!'

And Earth, still ready to spite Apollo if she could, took Daphne at her word and changed her into the first laurel tree.

Bitterly grieved at his loss, Apollo plaited himself a crown of laurels, crying:

'In memory of Daphne, this tree shall ever be sacred to me; my priests shall wear wreaths of it, and it shall crown the victors in all contests of music and song, and shall be the prize of those who triumph in all festivals held in my honour.'

Leaving the Vale of Tempe, where now laurels grew plentifully to join the other groves of trees, Apollo made his way back to Delphi. On the way he paused at the fountain of Telphusa and spoke to the river nymph:

'Telphusa, you tried to deceive me so as to keep this lovely place all to yourself. And you sent me to Crisa, knowing full well that the she-dragon Python lay in wait there to devour whoever she could catch—even if he were one of the deathless gods of Olympus. Keep your stream, if you will: but know that I will set up my altar above it, and those who come shall pause to pray, indeed—but to the Telphusian Apollo!'

So saying, he pushed down a great rock, so huge that it covered the glen through which flowed the stream, and set an altar of his own upon the high top of it. Then he turned back to the road which led to Delphi, and on rounding the spur of Parnassus a little before the Gorge of Castalia saw on the slope which had once been Crisa a noble temple standing completed.

'Trophonius and Agamedes!' he cried, when he had gone up by the Sacred Way and stood at the temple entrance near where the breath of sulphur, now hidden from sight, whispered up from the depths of Earth. 'You have wrought well indeed, and are worthy of all honour. Tell me now what you desire in reward, and I swear by Styx, the oath that none may break, that I will grant it—if it be a thing that mortals may receive.'

Agamedes and Trophonius consulted together; and then Trophonius said:

'Mighty Apollo, give to us that which you, being a god, know is the most desirable thing a mortal can receive.'

Apollo sighed. But he stretched forth the golden wand twined with ivy that he carried, which is called the *Caduceus*, and touched them each between the eyes with it. At once they sank down upon the hillside in sweet and happy sleep; but in a little while the sleep passed peacefully into death so gentle that neither knew when living ended and death began.

Yet afterwards Apollo prevailed upon grim Hades to release their spirits from the underworld, provided they never saw the light of day. And he made an oracle near where the stream of Telphusa was hidden under the great rock to consult which the pilgrims descended into a deep cave under the ground and were sucked into a hidden chamber where the spirits of Trophonius and Agamedes spoke to them, bringing them such messages as the gods deemed good for them to know.

But when these two left the earth, Apollo stood by his new temple at Delphi pondering on who should now be his first priests. For he had intended to bestow this honour on Trophonius and Agamedes.

While he pondered, Apollo looked out with his far-seeing eyes over all the length of southern Greece, and far out at sea, to the very south of the Peloponnesus, he saw a ship sailing on the wine-dark sea: a Cretan ship filled with men of Knossos, the city of Minos.

At once Apollo's mind was made up. Before the ship reached Greece he met it in the shape of a huge dolphin and sprang upon the deck. The sailors drew back in fear, for the creature was so huge that they could not cast it back into the sea, the home of fishes, and dared not try. Nor dared they loose the sheets or lower the sail, but left the oxhide rope untouched so that the ship sped through the waters unguided by them. But Apollo caused a wind to spring up from the south and carry the ship right round the coast of Greece, past Pylos where the Cretans had planned to put in, and up to Zacynthos and Ithaca, the islands outside the entrance to the Gulf of Corinth. There the wind changed and, blowing from the west, drove the ship up the narrow gulf until it came to harbour unguided by any man at the port of Crisa, where the plain below Delphi meets the sea. There the anchor stone was cast out untouched by visible hand, the sail was furled, and the great dolphin vanished.

Filled with fear the Cretans stepped ashore. And there Apollo met them, in the likeness of a young man, but far fairer than any of the sons of men. He seemed in the prime of youth, with broad shoulders to which the golden hair hung like a beam of light; his face was smooth and without hair, and it shone so that the Cretans knew they were in the presence of a god and knelt in awe before him.

'Strangers and guests,' said Apollo, for all strangers are guests to the Greeks, who have but the one word for both even to this day, 'you who once dwelt about wooded Knossos, but shall now return no more to your fairy city or your faithful wives, know that I am the son of mighty Zeus, and Apollo is my name. I have brought you over the wide gulf of the sea, meaning you no harm but rather great honour. For nearby stands my temple, newly builded, and it shall become the most famous in the world. The place where it stands is called Delphi, above the Oracle of Pytho; my name shall be known throughout all lands as the Pythian

Apollo; yet you shall pray to me as Apollo Delphinius, not only because you and your children shall be my priests at Delphi for ever, but also in remembrance of how, when I brought you hither, I took upon me the likeness of a dolphin [*Delphis*]. Moreover, as you make your way up the hillside to my temple, you shall sing the song which you learnt in your native Crete, the *Io Paean*, the "Hail to the Healer"—for I am the god of healing also.'

So the Cretans came up from the plain to beautiful Delphi, where Apollo's temple stood on the hillside beneath the tall cliffs of Parnassus and beside the Castalian Gorge, and they and their descendants became the priests of Apollo. And in each generation a woman of their race was chosen to be the priestess of his oracle. She was named the Pythoness in memory of the she-dragon Python, and sat upon the golden tripod over the mysterious breath of sulphur which inspired her to spreak strange and often riddling words of prophecy.

HERMES THE MASTER-THIEF

IN THE days when Cronos ruled, Atlas the Titan married
Pleione, daughter of Oceanus whose stream runs round the
earth. They had seven daughters, the nymphs called Pleiades,
who became the special attendants of the hunter-goddess Artemis.

The most famous of these was Maia, after whom the month of
May is named. For while she still dwelt upon earth, and before
she became a star, Zeus loved her. They were wed in secret among
the mighty hills of Arcadia in southern Greece; and there she bore
him a son called Hermes, whom she hid in a cave under Mount
Cyllene, in charge of the nymph who dwelt there.

From the moment of his birth Hermes showed that he was no ordinary child. On the very day he was born, when Cyllene thought that he was safely asleep, Hermes climbed quietly out of his cradle and slipped unseen out of the cave as swift and silent as a moonbeam. A little way down the hillside he came upon a tortoise and stopped to consider it.

'Yes, I see how I can invent a new and wonderful instrument of music,' thought Hermes. 'But I need a piece of oxhide and some gut.'

Even as he was thinking, he was scooping out the tortoise and polishing the shell, which he hid carefully. Then swift as quicksilver he sped across Greece on the look-out for cattle.

In Thessaly he found Apollo's herd—but no herdsman, for Apollo was still wandering alone in the Vale of Tempe, lamenting over the loss of Daphne.

The sun was sinking behind the high Pindus Mountains as Hermes paused beside Apollo's cattle with a sly smile. Quickly he chose out fifty of the best oxen, tied them together by the tails and began to drive and drag them backwards across Greece at an incredible rate. But first of all he made for himself a pair of strange round shoes of plaited osiers and myrtle twigs so that no footmarks might be left to show what manner of creature it was who had driven away the cattle.

Long before morning Hermes brought the herd of cattle to another great cave in Arcadia, in which he penned them. No one saw him as he passed, except for a crusty old peasant called Battus who happened to be sleeping in a ditch near Thebes and woke in time to perceive the amazing sight of the baby driving the cattle swiftly to the south; and at first Battus thought that he must have dreamed a very strange dream.

Once the cattle were safely penned in the cave, and he had fed them with armfuls of sweet lotus flowers and dewy galingale cut from the marshes by the River Alpheus, Hermes chose two and dragged them outside. With amazing strength he flung the two cows on their backs, killed them, skinned them and cut the meat into joints. Then he invented a new thing: cutting a stout laurel branch and trimming one end to a point, he spun it between his hands with the sharp end in a piece of softer, drier wood. Very soon a wisp of smoke arose, and presently the wood burst into flame: Hermes had made the first 'rubbing-sticks' to kindle fire by friction.

Swiftly he built twelve heaps of wood, set light to each and burnt on them the meat and bones in equal portions as sacrifices to the Twelve Gods—the most important of those who dwelt on Olympus and held rule in Heaven and upon the earth: Zeus, Hera, Poseidon, Demeter, Apollo, Artemis, Ares, Aphrodite, Athena, Hephaestus, Hestia—and, for the first time, Hermes himself.

Then, having cut what he needed from the skins and gut which he had kept, Hermes pegged out the rest to dry and hastened back to his home in the cave under Mount Cyllene, pausing only to collect the tortoise shell before slipping quietly back into his cradle and wrapping the baby-clothes about him.

A few days later it chanced that Apollo, wandering sadly out of the Vale of Tempe still grieving for Daphne, came upon his cattle grazing on the rich grass of the plain of Thessaly and discovered that fifty were missing.

Full of rage and distress, Apollo set out in search of the missing cows, scouring Greece from north to south, and offering rich rewards to anyone who could find them. In the wild and mountainous district of Arcadia, not far from Mount Cyllene itself, he met a band of Satyrs with their father Silenus—just such a band of these half-men left over from a former age as Prometheus had found in Arcadia when he first reached Greece with his gift of fire.

With great eagerness Silenus offered to find the cattle for Apollo, provided he was well paid for his services. Promising the Satyrs a long holiday from toil with as much food and drink as they wanted, Apollo left them to their search, while he continued on his swift way up and down Greece.

Now the Satyrs, as Apollo knew well, were full of boastings and big promises, but as lazy and cowardly as a host of monkeys. He had little hope that they would find any trace of the cattle, and felt sure they would soon give up the search. However, fortune favoured them on this occasion. Roaming among the mountains, they found first of all some cattle-tracks on the sandy shores of the River Alpheus, and then traces of the strange round basket-work footprints that Hermes had made both there and outside the cave on Mount Cyllene.

'Whatever monster has stolen Apollo's cattle must be hiding in the cave!' cried the Satyrs. 'All we need to do is to rush in and drag him out!'

'Splendid!' cried Silenus. 'In you go, and I'll wait here until you bring him.'

This was not at all what the Satyrs intended to do, and they began at once making excuses and edging away.

'It must be a very fearful monster!' they cried. 'Listen! It's in there now, making a strange noise!'

'Nonsense!' shouted Silenus, who was a bit deaf. 'What cowards you all are! If Apollo's cattle are in that cave I'll go in and drive them out. I'm not afraid of cows!'

Silenus advanced cautiously to the entrance of the cave, and then stopped suddenly. For now he heard the strange sounds which had frightened the Satyrs: sweet strains of music, but coming from an instrument which none of them had heard before.

This was too much for Silenus. Anything new must be terrible, and he began retreating hastily, exclaiming:

'There's nothing to be frightened of. I'd go in myself, but I've just remembered something I ought to do. So I'm off now; but you go in, and bring out the cattle, and win the reward.'

'You're not going until we know what's in there!' shouted the Satyrs, grabbing hold of Silenus. 'Let's make a terrible warlike noise. Then the monster will be so frightened that he'll come out and beg for mercy.'

Whether the noise they made was warlike or not, it succeeded in its purpose, and they were just getting ready to run for their lives when out of the cave came the mountain nymph Cyllene.

'What wild creatures are you?' she asked in her gentle, digni-fied voice. 'Why are you making such terrible noises and frighten-ing away all the birds and animals whose home is on my mountain here? Surely you would not dare to harm a nymph such as I, to whom the gods of Olympus have given this mountain in charge?'

'Stay your anger, stately nymph!' exclaimed the Satyrs. 'We do not come as enemies, nor mean you any harm. But tell us what the strange sounds are which come from your cave and fill us with amazement and wonder.'

'Now you are behaving like sensible creatures,' said Cyllene, 'and I will tell you everything. In this cave lies a wonderful child called Hermes, whose father is none other than Zeus himself, though his mother is only Maia the Pleiad, daughter of Atlas. I am his nurse, and truly I have never seen such a wonderful child. He grows faster than any child of ordinary parents; why, he is only six days old, but already he is more of a boy than a baby— almost a youth, indeed. As for the sound which frightened you so much, it is no more than a toy which the child Hermes has invented to amuse himself.'

'Tell us about the toy,' begged the Satyrs. 'It makes such a lovely, exciting sound.'

'Well, it is made out of an empty tortoiseshell,' said Cyllene. 'The baby has stretched a piece of newly flayed cow's hide over it, with seven strings made of cow-gut. He calls it a lyre, and he lies in his cradle playing happily with it for hours at a time.'

'Hurrah! Hurrah!' shouted the Satyrs. 'He must be the thief ! The cow's skin . . . where did he get it from? It must be this young Hermes who has stolen fifty of Apollo's cattle and driven them all the way from Thessaly to this cave.'

'What nonsense is this!' exclaimed Cyllene angrily. 'How can a six-day-old child drive a herd of cattle all the way from Thessaly, and kill and skin a cow? You had better be careful, saying a thing like this! First of all, the child you are calling a thief is the son of Zeus; and secondly, everyone will say that you have gone quite out of your wits to suggest such a thing.'

They were still arguing when Apollo arrived suddenly, and they all fell silent as the shining immortal strode into their midst, the golden wand in his hand.

'So you have found the thief after all?' he cried. 'He is in this cave: I know by those strange tracks. For near Thebes I met an old man called Battus who told me that he had seen a strange child with round basket-like sandals driving my cattle backwards so that the tracks pointed the wrong way. Had not Battus seen this and told me, I would have followed the footmarks to Thessaly—and found no cattle. I lost track of them among these mountains, it is true, but from time to time I came across the footmarks of the thief. And see, here they are, leading into this very cave!'

Apollo strode into the darkness, and in the light of his presence

it was dark no longer. He came to the cradle and looked down into it, and Hermes curled himself up in his baby-clothes and tried to look as small as possible. But Apollo was not deceived.

'Child, hiding in the cradle!' he cried. 'Tell me where my cattle are! Otherwise I will take you and cast you down into Tartarus, the prison in the lower world where the Titans lie chained, and no one shall ever set you free again.'

'Cattle?' lisped Hermes innocently. 'What a funny word! What does it mean? Something you've lost? Well, I am quite ready to swear a solemn oath—yes, even by Styx, the oath no immortal may break—that there are no cattle in here. And also that I have not seen or touched or done anything with things I've never heard of.'

'Rogue and deceiver!' cried Apollo, but there was no real anger now in his voice. 'I know well who you are—Hermes, my half-brother, the son of Zeus and Maia! You talk so innocently that I believe—that you are an expert thief of long practice! I know well that you have stolen my cattle; come with me to Olympus, and see if you can deceive Father Zeus himself!'

'Yes, take me before Zeus, you cruel son of Leto!' exclaimed Hermes. 'He will tell you how ridiculous it is of you to accuse a mere baby like me of stealing cattle—things I had not ever heard of until you mentioned them!'

So they made their way to Olympus, arguing as they went, Hermes always slipping through every argument and never quite telling a complete lie, and Apollo becoming more and more amused and captivated by this new and agile-minded brother.

At last they came to fragrant Olympus and stood on the golden floor before the throne of Zeus himself, where the other gods and goddesses sat round sipping the divine nectar which Hebe poured for them.

'Welcome, my son Apollo!' cried Zeus. 'We have lacked you all too long in Olympus. . . . But say, who is this child you bring with you, who has the very look of a herald, young though he is? It must be for some important reason that you bring him here before the whole council of the gods.'

'My father,' answered Apollo, 'I bring before you this child who is an expert thief, a burglar whom I found hiding in a cave under Mount Cyllene. He has stolen fifty of my cattle from Thessaly. His cunning is almost beyond belief, for he drove or dragged the cattle backwards all the way to Arcadia so that their footmarks should point in the wrong direction; and he invented round sandals of wickerwork for himself so that no tracker could tell in which direction he had gone. If he had not been seen by a man called Battus, who happened to be lying in a ditch near Thebes, I would have known nothing about it; but on this man's report of what he saw, and with some help from Silenus and the Satyrs, I have found and arrested the thief, young Hermes. All the way from Cyllene to Olympus he has been producing such good arguments to prove that he could not possibly be the culprit that he has almost persuaded even me!'

'Great Zeus—my father also!' exclaimed Hermes eagerly. 'Listen now to what I have to say. I am your son; my mother, Maia, brought me into the world scarcely a week ago. And with such a father and such a mother how could I possibly be suspected of theft? I will tell you the absolute truth—and indeed I cannot lie. This big bully of a brother of mine came charging into the cave where I lay, shouting that I had stolen his cattle, and threatening to throw me down into Tartarus. How can I possibly be guilty? A small child like me! I've sworn solemnly to Apollo; and I'll swear again now before you and all the deathless gods that I haven't got and have never had a single one of Apollo's cattle in my cave on Mount Cyllene—and indeed that I have not got the fifty cows which he says he has lost shut up in any cave anywhere.'

Then Zeus, who knows all, laughed aloud at the cunning and the craft of his son Hermes, laughed until the thunder rumbled merrily over the earth and the summer lightning flashed and spluttered across the sea.

'My sons,' he said to Hermes and Apollo, 'it is my will that this quarrel goes no further. Hermes, guide your brother to where *forty-eight* cows are hidden in a cave in Arcadia, and pay him whatever price may satisfy him for the two which are not there. Then, when you have paid your debts and made friends, you may both return to Olympus.'

Back to Arcadia sped Hermes and Apollo, but this time to the cave near the River Alpheus where the cattle were hidden. When Apollo saw the skins of the two slain cows pegged out on a rock, and had counted his herd and found that two were indeed missing, he turned upon Hermes in a fury, and began twisting tough willow withies to tie him. But Hermes slipped out of every knot; and the moment a withy touched the ground it took root and began to grow into a hedge.

At last Apollo gave up in despair, only to find that Hermes had now stolen both his golden bow and his quiver full of arrows, and hidden them too. But Hermes realized that he had gone far enough, for Apollo was now working himself up into such a divine rage that anything might happen. So he drew out the lyre, which he had kept hidden all this time in his cloak, and began to play softly and sweetly on it.

As the clear notes rang out the anger faded from Apollo's heart, and the beauty of the music swept over him and filled him with joy and peace.

'Son of Maia, what is this lovely thing on which you play?' he asked when Hermes paused at length. 'Though I lead the Nine Muses when they sing before the gods on Olympus, and am the partner of their songs and dances on Helicon and the high slopes of Parnassus, never have I heard music like this. If you will but give me this wonderful instrument and teach me to play on it, I will not only forgive you for the theft of my cattle and for the two which you have slain, but I will exchange for my bow and arrows which you have hidden this golden wand twined with ivy leaves. When this wand, which is called the *Caduceus*, is yours, you will become the herald and messenger of the gods of Olympus and pass freely from Heaven to earth, and even to deep Erebus, to the realm which Hades rules.'

Hermes laughed with glee and the bargain was struck. Then the two gods, having driven the cattle back to their meadow in Thessaly, set out together for Olympus, Hermes instructing Apollo as they went how to hold the lyre on his left arm and touch the seven strings with the key held in his right hand.

When they stood once more before Zeus, the father of gods and men welcomed them gladly and gave Hermes his rightful place in Olympus among the Twelve Gods. And seeing the golden *Caduceus* in his hand, he brought to pass all that Apollo had promised. For he gave Hermes winged sandals also and a herald's hat with wings, and appointed him messenger of the gods, and guide of spirits to the realm of Hades. He also made him a bringer of luck to mankind, as well as the patron of all cunning thieves, and the instructor of those who seek craft and guile, cunning in war, and wisdom in council; and he made him the guardian of shepherds.

PALLAS ATHENA

WHEN Zeus first began his campaign against Cronos and the Titans it was Metis, the daughter of Oceanus, whose wise counsel helped him most. It was she who showed him how to rescue his brothers and sisters whom the monstrous Cronos had swallowed; and she continued to assist him with her prudence and good advice until the war was won and the Titans were imprisoned for ever in Tartarus.

When the time came for Metis to receive her reward she

demanded nothing less than to be the wife of Zeus. This was before he married his sister Hera and made her queen of Heaven, so he consented, though not very happily. For Metis was one of the Titan kind, and although in the reign of Cronos she had been the goddess of prudence and good counsel, she had also magical powers such as that of changing herself into any shape she chose.

Naturally, when she became the bride of Zeus she took on the form of a beautiful goddess, and for a little while Zeus was happy with her and his fears were laid at rest—but not for long. The wise Titan Prometheus, who had also helped Zeus to gain the victory, and who was now busy creating mankind to people the earth, came to Zeus one day with words of warning. (For this was before Prometheus stole fire from the chariot of the Sun and suffered his terrible punishment on Caucasus.)

'Take care, great Zeus,' said Prometheus. 'I who have some power of seeing into the future, and who can hear and understand the words spoken by Mother Earth, have learned that if Metis bears children, the first will be a daughter—the wisest of all goddesses. But if she bears another child it will be a son who is fated to become the lord of Heaven.'

Zeus was sorely troubled at this, and realized why he had felt so much hesitation over marrying Metis. He knew that he was in great danger not only from the son who might be born, but also from Metis herself, who would never agree to cease from being his wife and, being a Titaness, with such strong powers of magic, would probably wreak some terrible vengeance on him if he tried to put her away.

Also he wanted his daughter to be born to inherit all the wisdom and wise counsel of Metis and to take her place among the new gods of Olympus.

At last he hit upon a strange scheme, which showed that he was still very much the son of Cronos the Titan. Whether or not it was Prometheus who told him how his daughter might still be born even after Metis was no more, and warned him of what he himself must suffer at her birth, Zeus proceeded with his plan.

As he and Metis sat together on mighty Olympus, looking out

over the wide world, Zeus brought up the subject of her magic power of changing from one form to another.

'Is there no creature too vast and strong for you to take on its shape?' asked Zeus. 'A lioness, for example?'

'That is easily done,' smiled Metis. A moment later she was gone, and a huge golden lioness stood in her place, roaring until Olympus echoed.

When Metis was herself again Zeus remarked: 'I should never have doubted that the queen of Olympus could take the form of the queen of beasts. But it seems to me harder for one so noble and mighty as you to become a small and worthless creature—a fly, for example.'

Scarcely had he spoken when Metis vanished and an ordinary-looking fly settled on his hand. In a moment Zeus had swallowed the fly—and that was the end of Metis.

But in swallowing her Zeus had swallowed all her wisdom, and her unborn daughter too—though her birthday was not yet. Indeed, before she was born Zeus had married Hera and made her the queen of Heaven instead of vanished Metis. Apart from Prometheus, neither gods nor mortals knew what had become of her, save only for Helios who drove the chariot of the Sun across the sky each day and saw everything that took place in Heaven or upon the earth.

About this time Zeus decided to divide the earth among the immortals, making one or another of them the special guardian of each district or island or site of a city that was to be. They cast lots on Olympus, parcelling out the whole earth between them, and in doing so forgot Helios himself, the only god who was not present, since none but he could drive the Sun-chariot over the great arch of the sky.

When night came and Helios had stabled his horses in his palace with the silver doors which Eos the Dawn-goddess would open for him in the morning, he hastened to Olympus, crying:

'Father Zeus, what land has fallen to my lot? For surely one of you remembered me and wrote my name on a shell to be drawn out of the golden urn with the rest.'

The gods were filled with shame and sorrow; and Zeus was ready to command a new lottery so that this time none should be left out.

But Helios exclaimed:

'There is no need to cast lots again, for there is one land, the most beautiful of all islands, which has not been given to any immortal. It lies still beneath the sea between Crete and the tip of Asia; for you, Father Zeus, plunged it to its doom to stamp out those wicked goblins the Telchines who dwelt there when Cronos ruled. Fighting on the side of the Titans, they made rain, hail and snow to vex the gods of Olympus, and had just invented a poisonous mist made of sulphur and the black water of Styx, the river of the dead, which would cause death to all living creatures and to the very trees and flowers, when their doom came upon them. Now, I beg you, raise up this island from beneath the sea and let me be its lord. If you do so, I will wed Rhode the daughter of golden Aphrodite, and make her the Nymph of the Island; and she, the Lady of the Roses, shall cover it with fair flowers and make of it the fairest isle in all the seas.'

'Bright Helios, be it as you wish!' cried Zeus. 'Now let the island of Rhodes rise out of the azure sea to be for ever the blessed kingdom of the Sun.'

All came to pass as Helios had asked and Zeus commanded. Very soon Rhodes was the envy of all the immortals: trees and flowers covered its hills and valleys; winter did not come near it, and the butterflies made their home under the shelter of Mount Atabyrios.

Helios and Rhode had seven handsome sons who grew swiftly to manhood and became the rulers of the island. And to them alone Helios told the secret of what had happened to Metis, and of the wonderful daughter who would soon be born with no visible mother.

'The moment she comes into the world I will see and tell you,' said Helios to his eldest son Cercaphus. 'As soon as I do, climb in haste to the top of Mount Atabyrios and sacrifice an ox to her; then you will be the first men on earth to do so, and she who is to be the goddess of wisdom and skill will be so pleased with you that she will grant you the fairest gifts she has to give, and bring good fortune to Rhodes for evermore.'

Cercaphus and his brothers had not long to wait. The day came when Zeus was troubled with a raging pain in his head. Knowing what this meant, he summoned all the immortals to Olympus, telling them that a new goddess was about to be born: 'A glorious goddess, bright-eyed, inventive, unbending of heart, pure virgin, saviour of cities, and most valiant.'

When all the gods and goddesses were assembled in Olympus, Prometheus came among them bearing a great axe. He went straight to the throne where Zeus sat, bowed low before the king of gods and men, and then, whirling up his axe, struck Zeus full upon the crown of the head with its sharp blade, for a moment splitting open his immortal skull.

There went up a great gasp from the gods and goddesses: and in that moment before the wound closed and was healed as if nothing had happened, there sprang a shining shape from the head of Zeus and stood before them all on the golden floor of Olympus. It was a tall and beautiful goddess, with flashing grey eyes, clad in shining armour and shaking a sharp spear. As Athena sprang from the immortal head and stood before Zeus all Olympus rocked, the earth trembled and the sea was troubled; bright Helios himself stopped his swift horses, and the Sun stood still in Heaven for a while.

Then Athena put off her helmet and armour, and Zeus and the gods rejoiced at her coming, and made her welcome to her place among them in Olympus.

Helios continued on his way across the sky; but he contrived to send a swift message to his son Cercaphus that the time had come to offer the first sacrifice to the new goddess in the sight of all men to gladden the heart of Athena and of almighty Zeus her father—and win her favour for Rhodes above all other lands.

Eagerly Cercaphus and his brothers set out for the top of high Mount Atabyrios, driving a fine ox for the sacrifice and carrying dry faggots of wood. When they came to the summit they built a great altar, heaped the wood upon it, slew and cut up the ox and prepared for the sacrifice. But a strange cloud of forgetfulness had lain over their minds; not one had thought to bring fire with them, nor the means of making fire. And so the sacrifice was incomplete, and no savour of burnt offering could rise to Olympus and make Athena turn a kindly gaze towards Rhodes.

The honour of making the first sacrifice to the new goddess which the sons of Helios failed to gain was won by a little village called Cecropia, built upon a great rocky acropolis which rose out of the plain of Attica a few miles from the sea, and thither in time Athena went to claim the site as the chief centre of her worship.

Zeus, however, did not let the sacrifice attempted by Cercaphus and his brothers go unrewarded, nor did Athena herself. Zeus caused a yellow cloud to pass over the island from which fell a shower of gold; and Athena bestowed upon all who dwelt there the gift of surpassing all mortal men in their deftness of hand. Soon the men of Rhodes were fashioning works of art—statues and pottery and gold shaped into cups of necklaces—more beautiful than those made anywhere else. And in days to come their descendants fashioned a statue of Helios, to stand beside the harbour, which for its size and beauty ranked as a wonder of the world and was called the Colossus of Rhodes.

Meanwhile Athena, though born fully grown and with so much of the wisdom of her mother Metis already hers, had certain things still to learn. For her upbringing she was entrusted to Triton, the son of Poseidon and his sea-bride Amphitrite. Triton was a merman who lived most of the time in the sea, and might be seen riding on a dolphin and blowing a great curved shell, or conch, like a horn. But he sometimes dwelt by a river in north Africa whose nymph, Trito, was his wife. They had a daughter called Pallas, and she became Athena's companion, and soon her close friend.

Together the two girls dwelt in the land of sunshine where the Lotus grew, where the river widened out into a lake called Tritonnis, and learned all those things that should be known by a goddess as well as by a mortal. They also learned to cast the spear and to wrestle. But one day they quarrelled, and Pallas snatched up a spear and made as if to cast it at Athena. Zeus was watching and sent a flash of lightning which dazzled Pallas and made her miss her aim; but Athena cast her own spear true to the mark, and her beloved friend sank to the ground and died.

Bitterly sorry for what she had done, Athena cried out that her friend's name should be linked with her own ever afterwards, and that men should pray to her henceforth as Pallas Athena. She also made an image of Pallas and set it up in Olympus. But later Zeus cast it down to earth to show Dardanus, his hero son—whose mother was Electra the sister of Maia, one of the Pleiades—where to build his city. Dardanus set up the image, which was called the Palladion, in the temple of Athena in his new city which was called Troy. There it became known as the Luck of Troy, and no one could conquer the city; until cunning Odysseus crept in during the siege and stole it, after which he made the famous Wooden Horse, by means of which the Greeks took Troy and destroyed it.

After the death of Pallas, Athena was ready to take her place among the Twelve Gods of Olympus and, like the rest of them, she demanded a city where she should receive special worship and honour.

'There is a village in Attica called Cecropia after its ruler,' she said. 'Of all places upon earth it was the first to offer me a burnt sacrifice, and that village is my choice.'

'It belongs to me!' cried Poseidon. 'It stands on a great rock a little way from the sea; but I have only to strike the ground with my trident and Attica will be flooded, making Cecropia into an island.'

Now it seemed likely that a great quarrel would break out between Poseidon and Athena; but to prevent it Zeus summoned a council of the rest of the Twelve Gods to decide between them.

They all met on the flat rocky top of Cecropia which rose out of the plain of Attica, with sheer cliffs on three sides and a steep slope at the narrowest end.

'Cecropia is mine!' cried Poseidon. 'It already belongs to the sea!' So saying he struck the rock with his trident, and at once there was a round well of salt water from which came the sound of sea waves whenever the south wind blew.

'Salt water will be of little use to the people of my city,' said Athena quietly. 'Though in time they may rule the waves, and then pay due honour to great Poseidon the Shaker of the Earth. But see now the gift which I make to them, which shall bring them both comfort and wealth, and to all mankind also.'

She touched the ground with her spear at a place where a hollow in the rock had become filled with earth, and at once the First Olive Tree pushed through the soil, grew to full size, and swelled until its trunk was thick and gnarled. Its branches put forth leaves of a beautiful greyish-green with undersides of silver, and then they began to bend and sag with thick clusters of ripe black olives.

'See!' cried Athena. 'Here is fruit for my people; and, when they crush it, clear rich oil that may be put to many purposes: they may cook their food in it; at night their lamps will burn brightly when filled with olive oil; and with it they may cleanse and anoint their bodies and make them fresh and supple.'

There was no doubt among the gods as to who had won the match. Poseidon went away in a whirlwind of fury, and raised a great tempest which flooded part of the land. But the result was only to give the people the wonderful natural harbours of Phaleron Bay, Piraeus and the Bay of Eleusis.

Meanwhile Athena changed the name of her city to Athens and set about making it the most famous in all the Greek world, and the most skilled in literature and architecture and sculpture. Where the great contest with Poseidon had taken place the Athenians of later ages built a beautiful temple of marble, called the Erechtheum, to cover the salt well and protect the divine Olive Tree. But on the highest point of the Acropolis they built the Parthenon, the temple of *Athena Parthenos*: Athena the Maiden, to be the most beautiful building, even in ruins, that the world has ever seen.

Before the golden age of Athens dawned, however, the earliest Athenians had much to learn. When Athena became goddess of the city the first ruler, Cecrops, had no son to succeed him, but only three daughters called Herse, Aglauros and Pandrosos. She made them her first priestesses, and they dwelt on the Acropolis in the earliest temple, the Royal House, which was built beside the well and the Olive Tree. Besides guarding and tending these, the three maidens learnt how to weave a beautiful robe by Athena's command to place on her statue when the time came for it to be set up.

One night Athena appeared to the maidens and told them to follow her. She touched the rock with her spear and a secret passage opened, leading down from the Acropolis by a steep stair. By this way she led them to the base of the rock and then on to the sacred garden of Aphrodite, where afterwards a temple stood. There she gave them a beautifully painted chest and told them to carry it back to the Acropolis by the way they had come, and guard it carefully in the Royal House.

'But do not open the chest,' she cautioned them; 'for what is inside it is not lawful for your eyes to look upon.'

The three priestesses bore the chest back by the secret stair up to the Acropolis and into the Royal House, where they guarded it as Athena had told them. But Aglauros and Herse were filled with curiosity to know what was inside. For a long time their fear of Athena kept them from disobeying her command; but at last they could bear it no longer. They tried to persuade Pandrosos to join them in their disobedience, but she refused indignantly. So they waited until one hot summer afternoon when Pandrosos was asleep, and then tiptoed to where the chest stood in the innermost shrine, and cautiously opened the lid.

Inside lay a baby boy, sleeping peacefully; and round him were curled two terrible serpents. At the sight of them and at the touch of the poisonous breath with which they hissed fiercely up at them, Herse and Aglauros went mad. Dropping back the lid they rushed screaming from the Royal House and flung themselves over the steep edge of the Acropolis and down on to the rocks far below.

At that very moment Athena was on her way to Athens, bringing a huge mass of rock to build up the one end of the Acropolis where there was a slope and not a sheer cliff. When she saw what had happened, she let fall the rock a mile away on the plain—where it stands to this day, and is called Mount Lycabettos.

But in spite of their disobedience Athena decided not to abandon Athens. So she herself, with the aid of Pandrosos, brought up the marvellous child, Erechtheus, who had been born out of the earth and reared by the two snakes. When he was a man, Athena made Erechtheus both her high priest and the first true king of Athens and the whole Attic plain. For Cecrops was dead, and he had ruled only over the little village which had now become the City of Athens. Erechtheus built a temple, the Erechtheum, on the site of the Royal House, and made the first and most sacred statue of Athena to stand in it. He also taught the Athenians to hold the great festival each year called the *Panathenaea* in honour of Athena, when the great procession wound its way up on to the Acropolis to present her statue with a newly woven robe.

Pandrosos had completed the first robe which she and her foolish sisters began; and ever afterwards the maiden priestesses of Athena followed her example. For weaving had been invented by Athena, and she had taught it to the three daughters of Cecrops, the first of all mortals to practise the art.

But after the First Web had been woven in the Erechtheum on the Acropolis of Athens, the art of weaving became known to mankind and spread over the world. Athena herself instructed her priestesses in other cities besides Athens, and indeed saw to it everywhere that women excelled in this her special art.

ROMAN

JANUS AND HIS CHILDREN

THE Romans conquered Greece and made it part of their
Empire; but the Greeks had already conquered Rome in
another way several centuries earlier. For northern Italy
was inhabited by the Etruscans, who had learnt much from the
Greeks; and southern Italy had many Greek colonies before
Rome was more than a little village by the Tiber. As the Romans
spread their rule over Italy and grew more civilized they took
over all the arts of the Greeks and their literature also, and with
them the myths and legends of Greece. They had gods and
goddesses of their own, but do not seem to have had many myths
or stories about them.

So they helped themselves to the whole of Greek mythology,
and all the Greek gods and goddesses, usually identifying them
with their own; changing their names, but keeping their stories.

For this reason it is almost as difficult to pick out the Roman
myths from Latin literature as it is to find the old Cretan myths in
the literature of Greece. Nearly all of the stories in Latin about
Jupiter or Minerva or Mercury are simply the Greek myths about
Zeus and Athena and Hermes.

Just occasionally we can catch a glimpse of the real old Roman
myths, particularly when the god in question had no real Greek

equivalent. Of these the first and the most important was Janus, the god with two faces who looked both ways at once, and who gave his name to January—the month which looks both to the old year and the new.

Before the world began there was a great chaos of fire, water and earth, and in the midst of it a ball of light which was Janus. Presently the elements drew apart and Janus took on the form of a god with a face on either side of his head. He looked above and below at the same moment, and the fire and the air shrank away in one direction to form the heavens, and the water and earth shrank in the other direction to become the world of man.

Then Janus stood upon the world looking before and behind at the same time, and the sea and the earth separated, so that the dry land rose above the ocean, which surrounded it but no longer mixed with it.

After that, at his touch, Tellus the Earth brought forth all living things, from trees and flowers and plants to birds and beasts and even mankind. From Earth were also born the rivers and the lakes, each with its own god or nymph. But Janus himself was the father of Tiberinus, the 'noble river' that was to flow 'by the towers of Rome'; and for many ages he dwelt upon the hill called Janiculum just across the Tiber from where Rome was to stand.

When Janus left the earth to take his place in Heaven he continued to be the guardian of the universe, though his grandson Jupiter ruled the sky and became king of the gods. For Janus closed and opened all doors: the door in the sky through which the rain came, and the doors by which Peace or War came forth to walk over the earth. And he himself sat at Heaven's gate, and even Jupiter could only pass in or out when he opened it for him.

While Janus still dwelt on earth and the gods moved freely among men, there came a ship sailing over the sea. In it sat what seemed an aged man with a white beard, carrying a sickle. Yet he had sailed from no earthly land, but from heaven itself, and came up the Tiber to anchor near the foot of the Janiculum.

Janus greeted him, saying: 'Welcome, great Saturn. to this most blessed of all lands. With you comes the Golden Age of peace and plenty. Now take to wife my daughter Ops, at whose touch the corn will push through the earth and the vines grow heavy with grapes—when you have taught men how to plant and sow; how to reap and thresh and grind the corn; and how to gather the grapes and tread them to make wine.'

So there was peace and plenty upon earth while Saturn reigned; the Seasons smiled, and men knew neither sin nor care. Nor did they need to labour, for what they did in the cornfields and the vineyards at Saturn's bidding did not seem a toil or a trouble.

During this happy time, when the immortals walked openly over the earth, mingling with mankind, there was a nymph of the woods called Carnea. She followed in the train of Diana the huntress, Jupiter's daughter, and might almost have been taken for Diana herself, except that she carried no bow or quiver of arrows, but only darts.

Many young men loved her, and even the gods came a-wooing. But Carnea would have none of them. Yet she never refused them, but said, when they came up to her in the forest or by the river: 'If you would have me, bring me to a cave where we may dwell, sheltered from the hot bright sun and also from the rain. Lead on and I will follow.'

Then the lover, filled with joy and gladness, would go ahead into one of the caves by Tiber's side, and Carnea would follow him—but not for long. For when he reached the cave and turned to take her by the hand, Carnea was no longer behind him but had run away and hidden in the bushes.

Yet she met her match at last. For Janus himself fell in love with her and asked her to be his.

'Then lead me to your cave,' she said as usual; 'for here the sun is too bright and dazzling.'

So Janus led the way to his cave beneath the hill of Janiculum, and Carnea would have run away as usual as soon as he turned his back on her. But two-faced Janus looked both ways at once, and so Carnea was never out of his sight, and there was no escape for her this time. However, when she knew that Janus, the greatest of the gods, was her lover, Carnea rejoiced and was glad that she had not been able to hide from him.

Carnea bore a daughter, as beautiful as her mother, but with a voice more sweet than any which had yet been heard. She was called Caneus, the singer: for when she sang the wild beasts and birds gathered round to listen, the streams stood still and the very rocks were moved by the beauty of her singing.

When the time came for Caneus to marry she became the wife of Picus, the son of Saturn, whom his father had made the first king of Latium, as the land by the Tiber was then called.

For Saturn had departed from the earth at last, and with him ended the Golden Age. Now wars and wrongdoings first came to plague the Italian land; there were masters and slaves for the first time, and rich and poor. But ever after, in memory of the days when Saturn reigned, a great festival called the *Saturnalia* was held for a week each December in which the slaves became free and did no work, while everyone made holiday with feasting, drinking and merrymaking.

When Saturn left the earth evil seemed to rise out of the ground and take many forms. Witches and wicked spirits appeared, and even one great monster who pursued Juno, the queen of Heaven, across the earth.

At this time Jupiter and Juno had quarrelled. After Saturn they became the chief of all the gods, ruling both Heaven and earth, and they had a son Vulcan, the lord of fire, who married Venus, goddess of love. But Jupiter made for himself a daughter called Minerva, and Juno was so jealous that she strode out of Heaven and wandered away over the earth.

She came at last to the most beautiful garden she had ever seen. All the flowers in the world seemed to be blooming in it, and there was no weed to be seen, nor did any blossom appear ever to fade or fall. Through the garden sparkled a crystal-clear stream of water, and the gentle west wind whispered among the leaves and petals bringing a glorious scent of flowers to greet the goddess.

Into this wonderful garden passed Juno and came to the palace which stood in the centre of it. There she was welcomed by a beautiful nymph who told her that her name was Flora.

'I was called Chloris once,' she said, 'and wandered free in the happy fields before the days of toil, while Saturn still reigned over the earth. I had no will to marry; but on a glorious day in spring Zephyr the West Wind saw and loved me. I fled, but he followed faster. He caught me in his arms and brought me hither, saying:

'"Be but my bride and you shall dwell in this garden and be called the goddess and queen of Flowers." So here we live in perfect bliss. But when my husband is away, ruffling the leaves and the growing crops with his gentle breath, I scatter the seeds of flowers over the earth, to bring peace and joy to all men.' Flora welcomed Juno into her palace and gave her fruit and honey and sweet wine made of flowers.

Then she said: 'Great daughter of Saturn, Juno, queen of Heaven, why have you come wandering to my door like this?'

'My grief cannot be comforted by words,' answered Juno. 'Since Jupiter scorns me and becomes a father without the need of a wife and produces a daughter who has no mother, what can I do? Surely nothing but wander over the world seeking some magic drug which will make me the mother of a child which has no father. To find that, and prove myself once more the equal of Jupiter, I will even venture by dark Avernus Lake down to Orcus, the land of the dead, where Februus grows richer day by day with the Manes and Lemures, the spirits of those who die, both evil and good.'

Then Flora hesitated, greatly fearing that if she helped Juno she herself would be punished by Jupiter.

'Fair nymph, you seem to know how to help me,' said Juno. 'Do not fear: I promise to hide from Jupiter the name of my helper and to see that no evil befalls you.'

'There is a magic flower in my garden,' confessed Flora. 'Nowhere else in the world is there one like it. I have but to pluck a blossom and touch a barren heifer with it, and at once she will become a mother and bear a strong and sturdy calf.'

Then, at Juno's prayer, Flora picked a bloom from the magic

plant and with it touched the goddess on the breast. And Juno thanked Flora and went on her way rejoicing; for she knew at once that her wish was to be granted.

Sure enough, in the distant land of Thrace where she hid herself, Juno bore a strong son called Mars. With him she continued her wanderings; for by now a monster called Typhon had risen out of the earth and was in pursuit of her and of her infant son.

One day Juno was resting under the shady poplar trees beside a wide river, and little Mars was playing with the pebbles on the bank. Suddenly there came a great rustling among the trees, and Juno sprang up, knowing that Typhon had overtaken her.

'Help me, nymphs of the river!' she cried, catching up Mars in terror, and springing into the water. At once two great fishes rose out of the depths and carried Juno and Mars safely away out into the open sea and across it back to Italy.

When they reached the Tiber once more and came ashore near the hill called Palatine, Jupiter met them and welcomed his wife and stepson, bidding them fear no more since he had overthrown Typhon and buried him for ever under Mount Etna in Sicily.

So Jupiter and Juno were reconciled; and in gratitude to the two fishes who had carried her and Mars to safety, Jupiter raised them to the skies as the constellation called *Pisces*—the Fishes.

But for a little while Mars lived on the Palatine Hill under the care of king Picus and his queen, Caneus the sweet singer; and there he grew to his full size and became the special protector of Rome, even when he had taken his place in heaven as the god of war.

While he dwelt on earth with Picus, Mars taught the people of Italy how to make not only swords but ploughshares too. And besides instructing them in the arts of war, he also showed them how to draw the curved blades of the ploughs through the earth and turn the sod before sowing the fields with corn.

Picus helped him in all things—but not always in his human shape. For a strange fate overtook Picus and separated him from his wife Caneus and their son Faunus.

One day as he galloped through the woods, two hunting spears in his hand, Picus met a beautiful witch who at once fell in love with him. Quickly she conjured up a phantom boar after which

the king rode, while she drew evil mists out of the earth in which his companions were soon lost.

Presently the boar came crashing through the thicket with Picus behind it, to where the witch stood. The creature vanished at a touch of her wand, and Picus drew rein not far away and looked about him in surprise.

'By those eyes of yours which have captivated mine,' cried the witch, stepping towards Picus, 'and by all your beauties, most handsome youth, which make me beg where I might command— look with love upon one who loves you! I am no ordinary woman: indeed I might call myself a goddess and claim dark Night and the bright Sun as my parents. So do not be hard-hearted; return my love, and great things shall be yours. But if you scorn me, be sure that my revenge shall be swift.'

'Whoever you are, I am not for you, nor ever can be!' cried Picus. 'Fair Caneus, the daughter of great Janus, is my wife, and her only do I love, and will for ever.'

'You will suffer for this!' cried the witch. 'If you scorn my love, you will never again speak to your Caneus.'

Picus turned and fled; but the witch waved her wand, shrieking spells after him, and on a sudden he was changed into the First Woodpecker. And all woodpeckers after him became the sacred birds of Mars and brought messages from him to those of his priests who could read the signs which they gave.

In vain for six nights and days Caneus sought for her husband up and down Tiber's side, over the hills of Palatine and Aventine, Capitoline and Esquiline, Caelian, Viminal and Quirinal—the seven hills on which Rome was soon to rise—and even beyond the river to Janiculum. Never again did she see Picus in this world; and at last she faded away, leaving only her voice to echo softly on the banks of Tiber.

But Picus and Caneus left a son, Faunus, who became the god of the woodlands, and the guardian of flocks and herds with command over the wolves who came out of the forests and down from the mountains to prey on them.

When Mars loved princess Silvia, their twin sons Romulus and

Remus were cast out on the bank of Tiber to die, by order of her cruel uncle Amulius, who would not believe that their father was a god. But Picus the woodpecker brought the news to Mars and at his request Faunus sent a great she-wolf to feed and protect the boys, so that they might grow up to found Rome, of which Romulus was the first king.

Wandering in the woods at the end of summer, Faunus met and loved Pomona, the nymph who tended the ripening fruit. But she would have none of him, nor of any wooers who came to seek her hand in marriage, even though all the sprightly young Fauns, the children of Faunus, pursued her.

Pomona cared for no man, nor for any god either. All her love was given to the fruits in her orchards; and when the Fauns threatened to capture her and carry her off to Faunus by force, she caused the apple trees to grow close together all round her, making a fence that could not be passed without her permission.

Yet she had one lover who entered without her knowing who he was. This was the kindly god of the turning year and the falling leaf, Vortumnus, from whom autumn draws its name. Often and often when he met her outside the orchard he took on some alien shape in hopes of winning her. Sometimes he came to her as a farmer with wisps of new-mown hay bound about his head; sometimes as an oxherd carrying his goad in his hand; sometimes as a vineyard worker, pruning-knife in hand, and again as a fisherman with his rod over his shoulder.

All these disguises were in vain; and at last he made himself into an old woman, in which likeness Pomona led him into her secret orchard and listened to his words of advice.

'You should marry,' said the pretended old woman. 'Look at the elm: if it stood alone and did not have the vine grafted on to it, what use would it be? Pretty leaves, perhaps, but no fruit. And if the vine were alone, unsupported by the elm, it would lie trailing on the ground and bear no fruit. So be like the vine, and take a husband.'

Pomona listened to the old woman's words, but shook her head. When, however, Vortumnus at length cast off his disguise and stood revealed in all his glory, she saw the truth of his words; for it seemed as if the bright sun shone suddenly through the clouds for the first time; and she knew love, which she had scorned when it had never touched her.

So Vortumnus and Pomona were married; and the trees put on their most glorious robes of red and gold and copper in honour of the marriage of autumn and the goddess of the ripening fruits.

PHRYGIAN

Attis and Cybele

In the land of Phrygia, which the Romans called Asia Minor and we now know as Turkey, the great mother-goddess Cybele, was born out of the earth on Mount Dindymos. As she lay on the hillside as a tiny baby there came out of the forest a lioness and a leopardess, who fed Cybele in turns as if she had been one of their own cubs, and guarded her from all harm.

When she grew older Dindymene the nymph of the mountain found her and tended her as carefully as if she had been Cybele's mother. Presently she led her to the court of Maeon, the king of Phrygia, and there the divine child grew into womanhood.

She was so beautiful that all the lords and princes of the land sought her hand in marriage. But Cybele would not wed. 'When the time comes for me to bear a son,' she said, 'that son will be born without a father.'

The Phrygians laughed at her, and king Maeon, thinking that she was but a mortal woman, was angry and declared that he would find her a husband forthwith.

But Cybele took up two round pieces of brass domed in their centres which Dindymene had made by her command, and clashed them together. At the sound of the First Cymbals there came two lionesses from the mountain and stood on either side of Cybele so that the king and people were afraid and turned to fly.

'Do not be frightened!' cried Cybele. 'I am the kindly one, the mother of all, born out of the Earth who is the true mother. I am the spirit of Earth, the goddess of all wild creatures, and of mankind as well. Now have no fear, but bring a chariot and harness these two servants of mine to the pole. For I must wander over the earth teaching mankind how to tame such wild things as will be useful to them: the ox and the ass, the horse and the sheep, and such others as may dwell in the lands which I visit.'

Full of awe, the king himself drew forth the royal chariot in which he was wont to ride, drawn by his slaves. Trembling with fear he and his princes harnessed the two lionesses to the chariot, and Cybele took her place in it and set out across the earth.

She was many years on her journey, and wherever she went she taught men how to tame the beasts that would be of most use to them. Whenever she left one land and travelled into the next young men who had become her priests went with her, leaping with joy, and clashing loud cymbals together so that all who heard might know that the great goddess Cybele had come among them to bring peace and plenty.

Yet though men caught and tamed the beasts, and learned to hunt the wilder ones for food, they did not know how to plough the fields and sow the corn; nor how to grow the vines and make the grapes into wine.

'This I am not able to teach,' said Cybele. 'But the time has come when one shall be born who will bring these gifts to the world.'

So she went away by herself to the deep valley of the River Sangarius, and there she came at length to where a tree stood in front of a cave. This was a magic tree, the First Almond in the world which Earth had sent up to be ready for Cybele when she needed it.

Cybele reached up and plucked the almonds and dropped them one by one into her bosom. And as each almond touched the breast of the goddess it vanished.

All through the autumn and winter Cybele dwelt in the cave, tended by lovely Sagaritis, the nymph of the almond tree; and

when spring was turning towards high summer she bore a son
called Attis.

Swiftly he grew to be the fairest of all men, so beautiful that
Cybele herself loved him, and lamented that he was her son and
could not be her husband.

'Come with me,' said Cybele, when Attis was full grown. 'For
you must follow me over the earth, teaching men how to plough
and sow, how to harvest and thresh the corn, how to grind the
grain and make the flour into bread. And you must also show
them the mystery of the grapes, the fairest of all fruit, growing on
the vines : yet, when the juice is crushed out of them and it seethes
and foments, it will become wine, to gladden the hearts of men—
but also drive them mad with ecstasy. But there is one thing you
must know : do not let love ever come into your heart, save only
such love as you feel for me, your mother. For if you do, a madness will come upon you more terrible than that which the juice
of the grape will ever bring.'

So Attis the beautiful set out on his mission, following where
Cybele led and teaching all the arts of the farmer and the wine-
grower throughout the whole land of Phrygia.

At last Cybele's task was completed, and she left the earth to
take her place in Heaven. Yet from time to time she returned to
Phrygia and passed once more in her chariot across the mountains. And in the wild places men might glimpse from time to
time the tall and stately goddess wearing her golden crown shaped
like a tower with turrets at the corners, and holding in her hand a
whip of knuckle-bones.

Attis still wandered the earth bringing more and more of
Phrygia under cultivation. But at last he too felt that his task was
accomplished. He did not, however, leave the earth as Cybele
had done. In spite of her warning, he felt his heart turning more
and more towards the beautiful nymph Sagaritis. He seemed to see
her more and more clearly in his mind, and was drawn towards
her so strongly that at last he set out for the River Sangarius.

At length he came to the cave where he had been born, beside
the almond tree now all covered with pink blossoms.

There he found lovely Sagaritis waiting for him. For she too
had fallen in love with Attis long ago when he dwelt in the cave,
and had waited there ever since, half hoping for his return, and
half fearing it.

'I have been sought in marriage, and loved to desperation by
the fairest women in Phrygia,' said Attis. 'Yes, and by nymphs
and goddesses as well. But never has my heart been touched by
love for any but you: never when they drew near has my body
trembled with desire as it trembles now that I draw near to you.'

'Remember the words of Cybele, your divine mother,' sobbed Sagaritis. 'Madness will come upon you if you dare to wed.'

'Let madness come!' cried Attis. 'One summer of your love is worth an endless winter without you!'

So they were married, and lived in perfect happiness through that brief bright summertide.

But when the leaves were turning to brown and falling from the trees, Cybele passing down the slopes of Mount Dindymos in her lion-drawn chariot saw Attis and Sagaritis standing together under the almond tree.

Then she knew that her warning had been disobeyed as it was fated to be. Filled with rage and jealousy she stretched out her whip and shook it towards them—and on the instant Attis was seized with madness and went rushing away up the mountainside screaming: 'Take away the whips! Beat me no more! Do not burn my flesh!' And on he went, hacking himself desperately with his wine-grower's curved knife as if to cut away those parts of his body which it seemed to him that the whip of Cybele had touched and charred.

Sagaritis, being a naiad, or tree-nymph, could not be harmed while her tree lived. But vengeful Cybele cut down the magic almond tree, and as it rotted away so Sagaritis faded and was no more.

But all that was mortal of Attis died upon the mountainside and his body decayed into the earth and brought far richer crops to Phrygia than to other lands. From the place where his body died grew the First Pine Tree; and soon Dindymos and all the mountains of Phrygia were covered with pine forests, the sacred trees of Attis.

Ever afterwards the priests of Attis and Cybele gashed their flesh during their mad dances in honour of the god and goddess when autumn was turning into winter. And ever afterwards the spring came and the new crops grew out of the earth—even as Attis had risen again, young and beautiful, to dwell with Cybele in heaven and wander the earth at her side bringing to mankind the new life of corn and vine, of flocks and herds and of all living things.

PERSIAN

MITHRAS, GOD OF THE MORNING

PERSIA, which Rome conquered, conquered Rome at the last in the person of Mithras whose worship spread over the Roman Empire even as far as Britain in the very last centuries of paganism, when Christianity was already claiming the whole civilized world.

The story of Mithras begins in ancient Persia in the earliest days of the world. Before the solid earth was made, the seas round it and the clear sky above with the great Sun passing across it each day in his chariot, there was only Zurvan.

Zurvan had no beginning and could not end, for he was Time. But he made the two great gods, Ahura Mazda (or Ormazd), and Ahriman, who created the world.

Ormazd made all things fair and beautiful above the ground, but Ahriman made for himself the kingdom of darkness and peopled it with demons. Soon he grew jealous of the lovely things which Ormazd was making on the earth, and set himself to spoil them as far as possible.

In the world of Ahriman it was always winter and the ground was hard and cold as if with ice. Where Ormazd ruled it was perpetual summer—until Ahriman brought two months of bitter winter each year to the upper world. Ormazd made Ghaon, the

Garden of Paradise, the most delightful place on earth: it was filled with roses, and among the trees sang birds with ruby feathers. But Ahriman created insects and snakes to bring trouble and decay in to the happy garden.

Then by the command of Ormazd the First Man and the First Woman, Mashya and Mashyoi, were born out of the earth fully grown. And Ormazd said to them:

'You are human beings, masters of the world. Think only what is good; do only what is good. Worship me, and do not listen to the Daevas, the demons of Ahriman.'

Then said Mashya to Mashyoi: 'He who speaks to us is the great god who made us. And by his will I am a man and you are a woman.'

After this they walked in Ghaon, the Garden of Paradise, and ate of the fruits, saying:

'It is Ormazd who has made the trees and the waters, the earth and the sun and moon and all other good things that we see.'

But Ahriman sent his Daevas to whisper to them, and presently they said one to another: 'Surely Ahriman made all things; let us worship Ahriman.'

Nevertheless Ormazd still watched over them and protected them so long as they did not give themselves wholly to evil. And they and their children lived in the Garden of Paradise, and there was a Golden Age for mankind.

But evil grew more and more among men who turned to Ahriman rather than to Ormazd. The Golden Age came to an end; the Garden of Paradise withered when Ahriman breathed upon it with his icy breath, and the descendants of Mashya and Mashyoi were scattered over the earth. Now they began to fight and slay one another just as Ahriman intended; in this way death came to earth, and each man and woman who died went down to dwell in the cold land of the dead where Ahriman was king.

Ormazd looked out upon the world in sorrow, pondering how he might win back mankind. At last he decided to end the First Men and bring into the world a new god of light who would make a new race.

At his command a great rock opened and a wonderful child stepped out, to the amazement of the shepherds who were grazing their sheep on the hillside. As darkness fell two of the shepherds stood on either side of the cleft in the rock, holding torches; and they saw the child grow into a young man who wore a cap on his head shaped like a blunted horn, wore a short sword at his side and carried a bow and arrows.

In the morning Mithras was full grown and ready to conquer the world. He clad himself in a garment of fig leaves and, setting an arrow to his bow, challenged Mitra the undying Sun himself. And Mitra guided his Sun-chariot down on to the earth, and the fire made an end of the men of the Golden Age and of many living things on the earth, both animals and trees and crops—but not all.

Out of the men of the Golden Age, the descendants of Mashya and Mashyoi, Mithras saved only the two shepherds, Cautes and Cautopates, who had held torches at his birth out of the rock. Them he hid in a cave deep under the ground, the first temple of Mithras, and they became the first holders of the Third and Fifth Degrees in the Grades of Mithras—the Soldier and the Persian.

Meanwhile shining Mitra with his golden crown of bright rays brought his four fiery horses to a stand and sprang from his chariot, whip in hand.

'Greetings, bright driver of the heavenly chariot!' cried Mithras. 'You who bring light and warmth to the earth will surely help me in my great work. Ormazd the Father has sent me to remake the world and people it anew. I am Mithras, and all men who follow me and take part in my sacred Mysteries shall triumph over the snares of the Daevas; and when they die Ahriman shall catch in vain at their souls. For Ormazd has prepared a Heaven for them—a new Garden of Paradise that is not of this world and to which Ahriman and his demons cannot come.'

So saying Mithras took Mitra by the hand; and bright Mitra knelt to him and did him homage, while Mithras set his own cap on his head for a moment, saying:

'For ever after this day the men who take part in my Mysteries and come to the Sixth Grade shall be called Heliodromes—drivers of the Sun-chariot—after you. And there shall be only one grade higher, the Seventh Grade, which shall be named Pater—the Father; for Ormazd alone is greater than Mitra.'

When Mitra had returned to his Sun-chariot and was driving once more through the sky, Mithras stood upon the burnt hillside and raised his hands in prayer to Ormazd. And Ormazd caused the rock to gape once more and let forth a Bull, greater, stronger, more filled with life and power than any bull seen on the earth before or since.

Flinging down his bow and arrows Mithras set out to capture the Bull. Stealing up behind it unseen he sprang upon its back and brought it to the ground. Then a terrible struggle took place; but in the end Mithras caught the Bull by all four legs and carried it away slung over both shoulders as a shepherd carries a lamb.

Yet once the Bull broke away, and would have escaped had not Mithras leapt on its back once more and caught it by the horns. When at last it fell exhausted he seized it by the hind legs and, setting these over his shoulders, dragged it away to the mountain beneath which was the sacred cave where Cautes and Cautopates had hidden from the burning heat of the sun.

Mithras would have tamed the Bull and stabled it in the cave.

But there came to him Corax the Raven, after whom the First Grade in the Mysteries was named, and said to him:

'I am sent to you as a messenger from Ormazd. He bids me tell you to draw your sword and slay the Bull as the first sacrifice of Mithras. For from his death life shall come.'

Mithras was sorely grieved to slay so beautiful a creature, and his face was full of sorrow as he forced the Bull to its knees, knelt on its back holding it by the upper jaw and plunged his short sword into its body behind the shoulder straight to its heart.

As it died a dog, a snake and a scorpion, the evil creatures of Ahriman, crawled out of the earth to drink its blood. But Mithras drove them away, and the blood of the Bull sank into the earth, and the fierce rays of the sun melted the Bull's flesh until it also entered into the ground.

From this sprang the new race of men and new life all over the earth. The First Man brought into being by Mithras was called Nymphus—the Bridegroom—and after him was named the Second Grade in the Mysteries of Mithras.

As the new men grew upon the new earth Ahriman tried again and again to destroy them. But Mithras sped hither and thither chasing the evil beasts such as the wild boar which Ahriman sent to slay, and shooting them down with his arrows. He tamed the dog and the snake to hunt with him, and his chief companion was the Lion, after whom the Fourth Grade in his Mysteries was called Leo.

Once Ahriman sent a bitter winter to freeze the earth and all upon it to death. But Mithras taught men to make sacred caves under the ground, like that which Cautes and Cautopates had made into his first temple, and shelter in them with their sheep and cattle.

Another time Ahriman dried up all the rivers upon earth, and both men and beasts were like to die of thirst. But Mithras fitted an arrow to his bow and cleft the rock with it so that fresh water gushed out and filled every spring and brook and river once more.

At last the time came when Mithras must leave the earth, and he called to him Cautes and Cautopates, his first priests, the two

surviving men of the Golden Age, in whose lives the life of an
ordinary man was but as a day.

'I must go now', he said, 'to join Ormazd in Heaven. But I will
continue to guard and guide all men on earth who worship in my
temples and take part in my sacred Mysteries. Not all shall pass
through the Seven Grades, yet all should seek to do so. For the
First Grade of Corax is for those who have heard my teaching
through the voice of my priests and wish to follow it; the Second
Grade makes a man Nymphus, for he is wedded to my faith; Miles
the Soldier comes third, since he fights for me, and Leo the Lion
hunts at my side to drive evil away, while Perses the Persian burns
out evil with his flaming torch and lights my follower on his way.
The Sixth Grade, Heliodromus, assures my follower that he shall
ride in the Sun-chariot at the last, when death takes him from the
earth, and he shall come to join the Father of Life at my table in
the Garden of Paradise, which I go now to prepare and keep for
him, and for all who keep the laws of Ormazd which I have taught
you.'

Then Mithras entered the first and greatest of his temples as the
Sun set; and there Mitra, having stabled his horses under the earth
with the Sun-chariot, came to join him. Together they feasted on
bulls' flesh, while Corax and Leo, Nymphus the First Man, Cautes
the Soldier and Cautopates the Persian waited on them, pouring
wine into bulls' horns like which the cap which Mithras wore was
shaped.

When the morning was near Mithras rose and said to his
followers:

'Slay the bull and feast in my temples under the ground even as
I have feasted, and be that your sacrifice to me for ever more, and
my pledge to you that you my worshippers shall pass as I am
about to pass, with the rising sun, to be with me for ever in the
Garden of Paradise beyond this world.'

After this Mithras was seen no more in the land of men, for he
had passed to the sky in the shining chariot of the Sun, bringing a
new morning of hope to all his followers on earth.

SCANDINAVIAN

ASGARD AND THE GODS

FAR away from the rich, warm, beautiful world of Greece and Rome, of Egypt and Babylon, on the very edge of the Roman Empire, lived the Northmen—the inhabitants of Scandinavia and Germany—the Danes and Saxons who conquered Britain and settled there and in Iceland and even planted colonies in north America.

To people living in the cold north lands, some even above the Arctic Circle, the world seemed a grim, rather terrible place, with the long bitter winters of ice and snow, fog and storm, and the brief bright summer all the more precious in consequence.

The men of the north had to struggle all their lives to win a living from the soil, to keep at bay the fierce packs of wolves from the mountains, and above all to defend themselves from bands of raiders who came to destroy their homes and carry off their wives and daughters and goods. And often they became Vikings themselves and went raiding other settlements of their own people, or of less warlike neighbours in Britain or Normandy or the Netherlands.

Like themselves, their gods delighted in battle and great deeds of bravery; and they too were at constant war with the Ice Giants and the Frost Giants, and looked forward to Ragnarok, the Last Great Battle—in which it seemed only too probable that they themselves would be defeated and the powers of evil gain control of Earth and Heaven.

The world itself (so the Northmen believed) had been born out of the ice and rime. In the beginning there was no land, only Ginnungagap—the yawning gulf. Yet at the north of it was Nifelheim, the shadowland of absolute cold; and far to the south was Muspelheim, the region of fire, guarded by the fire-demon Surtur. Between the two Ginnungagap was filled with rolling vapour and frozen air which at last drew together and formed Ymir, the First Giant, whose children were the Hrimthursar, the Frost-giants. He was utterly wicked, as were all Giants after him.

As Ymir stood in Ginnungagap a second creature came into being, made also out of frozen vapour. This was the cow called Audhumla, whose milk made the great rivers of life which fed Ymir. Audhumla licked the stones which were covered with salt and hoar frost, and from them grew Bur who was the father of Bor who married a Giantess and so became the father of the gods Odin, Vili and Ve.

The three gods slew the Giant Ymir and dragged his body into the middle of Ginnungagap. From it they made Midgard, the world in which men dwell. His body formed the earth, his icy blood melted and became the sea; from his bones grew the mountains and from his flesh the fertile soil. The skull of Ymir was set over the earth to form the great dome of the sky with his brains floating about in it as the first clouds; and fire drawn from Muspelheim made the sun, the moon and the stars.

To hold all in place Odin caused the great ash tree Yggdrasill to grow. Its roots were in deepest Nifelheim; its trunk held up Midgard, the world of men, and its branches arched over the sky to support Asgard, the land of the gods.

Out of two chips of wood from Yggdrasill which were cast up on the shore in Midgard Odin formed the First Man and the First Woman, whose names were Ask and Embla. Odin breathed the breath of life into them, while Vili gave them the powers of thought and motion, and Ve caused them to see and hear and speak.

Now Odin became the all-father of gods and men, marrying Frigga, daughter of the mountains, who bore him the great gods Thor the thunderer, Tyr the war lord, Bragi the minstrel, Uller the archer, Heimdall the guardian of Bifrost—the rainbow bridge between Heaven and Earth—beautiful Baldur the shining god of the sunlight, and others of less renown.

There were also the three Vanir: the powers of peace who grew out of the summer air. Niord guarded all living creatures, his son Frey taught the arts of agriculture, and his daughter Freya was the goddess of love and beauty. Niord dwelt far from Asgard, by the sea-shore; but Frey and Freya came to join the Aesir—the gods of Asgard—and Freya married Odur, one of the sons of Odin.

The strangest inhabitant of Asgard was Loki, the Fire-god. He was one of the Giant race, but forswore their evil ways and became Odin's blood-brother, swearing most solemnly to use all his Giant skill in the service of Asgard. And for a long time he was faithful to the Aesir, showing his kinship with the Giants only by the tricks and pranks he would play, even on the highest gods. At first these were innocent enough, and caused much mirth in the halls of Asgard. But gradually Loki's Giant nature began to get the better of him and his tricks became crueller and more evil, until at last he became the secret enemy of the gods, the traitor in their midst fighting on the side of the Giants.

There was some excuse for Loki's first plot against Asgard. One day he accompanied Odin and Odin's brother Honir, the messenger to mankind, on a visit to Midgard. For Odin went frequently in disguise among men teaching them many things, and punishing those who did evil. And when he could not go himself he sent Honir to be teacher and guide.

On this occasion the three gods wandered far over the earth, and as night was falling found themselves in a lonely valley of the mountains where no house was to be seen. Presently they came upon a herd of cattle, and as they were very hungry Odin told Loki to kill one of them and roast it for supper.

Loki did as he was commanded, and soon an ox was cut up and roasting merrily on great spits over a roaring fire.

'That meat must be cooked by now,' said Odin at last.

Loki went to look. What was his amazement to find the joints as red and raw as when he had cut them from the ox!

Loki stoked up the fire and they waited once more. At last he went to look at the meat again, and it was still as raw as ever.

'There is evil magic at work here,' said Odin.

As he spoke there was a sound of harsh laughter above them, and looking up they saw a huge eagle perched on a rock.

'If you will give me my fair share of the meat I'll see to it that it roasts quickly!' screeched the eagle.

The gods agreed to this, and the eagle flew down and fanned the flames with his giant wings for a few minutes, while the meat sizzled merrily.

As soon as it was well cooked the eagle said: 'I'll help myself first!' And with that he seized a shoulder in each claw and a leg in his hooked beak and prepared to fly off with them.

'You've taken too much!' cried Loki, who had a tremendous appetite; and in his anger he snatched up a heavy stick and struck the eagle on the back. At once the stick stuck to the eagle, and Loki found that he was stuck to the stick.

Off flew the huge bird, dragging Loki after it, and trailing him over the sharpest rocks and thorniest thickets it could find.

Loki shouted in vain for help, and begged the eagle to release him.

'That I will only do on my own terms,' said the eagle. 'I am Thiassi the Giant of the Winter, wearing my eagle-cloak with which I bring the storms. And I will drag you like this until you are torn to ribbons, unless you promise to give me Iduna and her magic Apples of Youth.'

'How can I?' gasped Loki. 'The gods of Asgard would never forgive me if I stole Iduna and her Apples. She was born out of the earth, bringing the magic fruit with her, and dwells always in Asgard, married to Bragi the minstrel. Each day the Aesir eat of the Apples and their youth returns to them; nor do the Apples ever grow fewer. How can I steal Iduna or the Apples?'

'Then you shall be torn to pieces!' screamed the eagle. 'All I

ask is for you to persuade Iduna to come down out of Asgard,
bringing the Apples with her. Once she is on the soil of Midgard
I can seize her and carry her off to my castle in Jotunheim, the
frozen kingdom of the Giants. . . . That is all I ask. Choose life
or death.'

At last Loki swore solemnly to betray Iduna to Thiassi; and
the eagle carried him back to his companions, released him from
the stick, and flew away carrying his share of the feast.

Loki said nothing to Odin and Honir about his bargain, nor did
he tell them that the eagle was really Thiassi. And although Odin
suspected that the eagle was one of the evil powers in disguise, he
thought that it had merely punished Loki cruelly for striking it.

Loki did not forget his oath to Thiassi. After much thought he
went to Iduna and said:

'Beautiful goddess of youth, are there other apples such as
those which you give each day to the Aesir and the Vanir who
dwell here in Asgard?'

'I do not believe there are other apples such as mine,' answered
Iduna. 'For kind Mother Earth gave them to me when I first came
out into the light, bidding me guard them always and give them
only to those who dwell in Asgard. Only those to whom I give
them shall have eternal youth; and they must never be given to
one of Giant race, nor to the Dwarfs who dwell under the earth—
not even to Evaldi the Earth Dwarf, my father.'

'Strange,' mused Loki; 'for there is a grove of apple trees not
far from where the lower end of Bifrost Bridge rests on the earth.
These apples are just such as those in your golden casket; and the
men of Midgard have found them. Soon they will taste the wondrous fruit, and remain young for ever, even as the gods.'

'That must not be!' exclaimed Iduna anxiously. 'Lead me to
this grove at once, for I must see whether the apples of which you
speak are of the same growth as those in my casket.'

So Loki led Iduna down over the rainbow bridge out of the
safety of Asgard and on to Midgard where Giants could roam
unseen. And, in her eagerness, Iduna feared no evil but carried her
magic Apples with her in their golden casket.

As soon as she was hidden among the trees, Thiassi in his eagle-robe swooped down and carried her and the Apples of Youth away to Thrymheim, his castle in the frozen land of Jotunheim where the Giants lived.

'Fair Iduna, be my bride and give me your Apples to eat!' cried Thiassi, throwing off his disguise as soon as she was safely shut in his highest tower.

'Never!' said Iduna bravely. 'None but the gods of Asgard may eat of my Apples—and they lose all their power unless I give them freely.'

'Then here you stay until you change your mind!' roared Thiassi; and swinging his eagle-cloak about him he flew out of the window and went rushing over the earth in a great storm of rage, bringing havoc and destruction wherever he passed.

In Asgard Iduna was sorely missed. Old age began to touch even the gods: Odin grew wrinkled, Thor's arm was not so strong, and strands of grey showed even in Baldur's golden hair.

No one knew what had become of Iduna. Bragi wept for his lost wife, singing only laments and dirges, and drawing melancholy notes from his harp. Odin sent out his swift messengers, the ravens of Hugin and Munin, who perched on his shoulders as he sat on his high throne looking out over the world; but for a long time they had nothing to report.

At last, however, they brought news that Iduna was held captive in the high tower of the castle of Thrymheim in the land of the Giants.

'That is Thiassi's castle,' croaked Hugin.

'Thiassi flies wrathfully about the world in his eagle-cloak,' croaked Munin.

'Just as he flew that day when the ox would not roast,' croaked Hugin.

'The day when he dragged Loki over the sharp rocks,' croaked Munin.

'Until Loki made his peace with Thiassi. . . .' croaked both ravens.

Now Odin began to suspect what had happened, and sent for Loki, who confessed all.

'I cannot blame you overmuch for buying your freedom from cruel pain,' said Odin gravely. 'But you must find a way of bringing back Iduna and the Apples of Youth to Asgard—and of punishing Thiassi, the Giant of the Winter.'

'The Lady Freya has a magic cloak,' said Loki. 'Whoever wears it takes on any shape he chooses. If she will but give it to me, I'll fly as a falcon into Thrymheim and bring back Iduna.'

Freya willingly handed her cloak to Loki, who set out at once in the shape of a falcon, and flew to Thiassi's high castle in Jotunheim. The Giant himself was out fishing, so Loki slipped safely in through the topmost window, where he found Iduna pale and troubled, but still refusing to part with her Apples.

When Loki flung off Freya's cloak and assumed his own form Iduna greeted him eagerly, and begged him to carry her back to Asgard.

So Loki turned her into a sparrow and himself back into a

falcon. Then he seized her carefully in his claws and set out for
Asgard.

It was not long, however, before Thiassi discovered what had
happened. Wild with rage he donned his eagle-shape and flew
off in a blast of wind so deadly that nothing remained standing on
the earth beneath his flight.

Far away in Asgard the gods waited eagerly. Presently far-
sighted Heimdall cried:

'I see the falcon flying this way with a sparrow in its claws.
But behind it comes a great eagle, and the earth grows black with
the cruel cold beneath the beat of his wings!'

On the very rampart of Asgard the gods made haste to prepare
a great heap of pine-chips soaked in resin, and stood ready with
torches in their hands. With a last desperate effort Loki skimmed
into Asgard and fell exhausted to the floor. The moment he had
passed over the heap the gods cast their torches into it and a great
flame shot fiercely up. Thiassi was close behind Loki, flying so
fast that he could not stop or turn. The fierce flames set fire to his
feathers so that he fell to the ground, and the gods slew him with
their swords and axes on the very threshold of Asgard.

Then they turned, to find Iduna standing ready for them with
the Apples of Youth in her hand. And when they had eaten, their
youth returned to them, even as it returns to the world each
spring when winter has been defeated and is dying in the beams
of the summer sun.

Loki was forgiven now that Iduna and her Apples were safe in
Asgard once more, nor did anyone yet suspect him of siding with
the Giants. Yet already he was leaning more and more towards
his own race; for even as he flew over Jotunheim to rescue Iduna
his eyes fell on a young Giantess called Angurbodi, and he fell in
love with her.

So he stole away from Asgard more and more often to visit his
Giant bride in Jotunheim; and three terrible children had been
born to them before Odin realized what Loki was up to. When he
did, his wise heart was filled with trouble and foreboding, for his
great wisdom, which he had purchased from the Giant Mimir in

exchange for one of his eyes, told him that the three children of Loki would be among his deadliest enemies at Ragnarok.

As they were the children of his blood-brother, he could not slay them. But he sent Thor and Tyr to bring them to Asgard. The two gods set out in Thor's chariot drawn by goats, and the thunder roared and the lightning flashed as they sped across the sky by the roadway of the clouds.

When they returned, the gods gathered in horror round the three monsters whom they brought with them.

At once Odin took the second of these, a huge serpent, and flung him into the sea, where he grew so fast that at length he encircled the earth and could hold his tail in his mouth. Having disposed of Jormungand, the Midgard serpent, he turned to Loki's youngest child Hela, half of whose body was that of a woman and the other half that of a decaying corpse, and sent her down to Nifelheim below the earth. There, at his command, she became queen of the dead, and a great wall was built round her realm, which was known as Helheim.

As for Loki's eldest child, the wolf Fenris, Odin thought at first to keep him in Asgard and train him to hunt and fight for the gods. But Fenris grew so fast and became so ferocious and cruel that at last it was decided to bind him in chains.

'Show us how strong you are!' cried Thor when the chain was ready. 'I'll tie you up with this pretty toy, and we'll see how easily you can break it.'

'Agreed!' smiled Fenris, looking scornfully at the chain. 'That's a mere cobweb to me.'

When Thor had bound him as firmly as he could, Fenris proved his words true. He yawned, he stretched—and the chain flew into small pieces all round him.

'You must make something stronger than that!' barked Fenris.

The gods tried again; but once more Fenris, putting out his vast strength, scattered the huge iron links all about him.

Then the gods took council; and Odin sent messengers to the Dark Elves who lived under the earth and who were skilled above all creatures both in smiths' work and in magic. It was they who had made Thor's great hammer Miolnir, which always returned to his hand however far he flung it at an enemy; and the spear Gungir for Odin, which never failed to hit its mark; and the gold ring Draupnir, from which eight rings of equal value fell on every ninth night. Now they forged the chain Gleipnir of thin shining steel, tempered in a magic brew made from the noise of a cat's footfall, the beards of women, the roots of stones, and the breath of fish—since when cats have made no noise, women have not grown beards, stones have lost their roots and fish no longer breathe.

When Fenris saw the chain Gleipnir he sniffed at it suspiciously, for it was as smooth and thin and soft as a thread of silk.

'There is magic in this,' he said doubtfully. 'I do not trust any of you. . . . But I will let you bind me with Gleipnir if, as a pledge of good faith, one of you will put his right hand in my mouth while I am breaking the chain.'

Now the gods hesitated, as well they might. But brave Tyr stepped forward and thrust his hand between the wolf's huge jaws. Then the rest bound Fenris with Gleipnir and drew the end of it through a rock. Struggle as he might, Fenris could not break the chain which bound him, and he was doomed to lie fettered in it at the world's end until the day of Ragnarok.

But Tyr lacked a hand ever afterwards.

It was after the binding of Fenris that Odin began to make ready for the day of the Last Great Battle. Up in Asgard he built a mighty hall called Valhalla, and decreed that all men who fell in battle should not go like other humans to the dark land of Helheim but come in triumph to feast in Valhalla and dwell there until the time came for them to form his army.

Now wars flourished in Midgard, and every man who could became a warrior and hoped to die in battle. And Odin sent out his daughters the Valkyries, the 'Battle-choosers', to ride over the fields of war and choose all those who had died bravely. Then they rode back to Asgard carrying the chosen, and the feast was made ready in Valhalla for Odin's army, the Einheriar.

Every warrior who became one of the Einheriar found himself

young and strong and healed of his wounds by the time he reached Valhalla. There the feast was spread each night, with roast pork in abundance and as much mead as they could drink. The Valkyries waited on them, having doffed their helmets and laid by their swords and shields; and no matter how much the Einheriar drank, they rose next morning fresh and clear-headed. All day long they rode and fought in the great meadow before Valhalla, hacking each other to pieces in glorious battle—yet appearing at the evening feast whole and unwounded. Each morning the cook Andhrimnir slew the great boar Saehrimnir and boiled his flesh in a huge kettle, and each morning he was alive and whole again, ready to be killed and eaten once more. Nor was there ever a shortage of meat, though Valhalla had five hundred and forty doors, by each of which eight hundred heroes might come in or out at once. Nor was there ever any lack of mead, which the goat Heidrun yielded instead of milk.

At night Odin would sit at the head of the banquet board in Valhalla, sipping his mead, but throwing his share of meat to his two wolves Geri and Freki—for the gods of Asgard did not need to eat, save only the Apples of Iduna; though when they went among men or giants they ate meat with the best, Thor and Loki being particularly famous for their appetites—which led them once into a contest with the Giant King of Jotunheim. In this they were defeated only because Loki was set to eat against the Fire Giant, and Thor to drink from a huge horn, the other end of which reached the sea—which ebbed for the first time, before Thor ceased from drinking and the tide came in again.

By day Odin went more often than ever in disguise to Midgard seeking fresh warriors to join the Einheriar in Valhalla, and training the sons of kings and the bravest of fighting men to become such great heroes as Sigurd the Volsung and Gunnar of Lithend and Grettir the Strong, whose deeds and deaths are told in the stirring words of the great Icelandic sagas. For the time was drawing nearer and nearer when the powers of evil would rise up to destroy the earth and invade Asgard, when Ragnarok, the day of the Last Great Battle, should dawn.

THE DEATH OF BALDUR

BRIGHTEST of the sons of Odin was Baldur the beautiful, with his golden hair and the morning sunshine in his face. He dwelt in Asgard in his shining palace of Breidablik with its silver roof and pillars of gold, and was gay and happy with his young wife Nanna and their son Forseti the law-giver.

In front of Breidablik stretched the shining meadow of Idavollr, where day by day the younger gods met for their sports and exercises—casting the javelin and throwing the shining metal disk. Here would come Hermodur the swift-footed and Vidar the silent; Heimdall the watchman of Asgard, who could hear the grass growing in the fields and the wool on the sheep's backs; Bragi the sweet singer and Uller the bowman; and Baldur's twin brother Hodur, whom he loved best of all the sons of Odin— Hodur the dark and sad, who had been born blind and was the god of night as Baldur was of the day.

At last there came a time when a shadow seemed to fall over Baldur; he no longer smiled, and his eyes grew anxious and full of trouble. When Odin learned of this he called together all the gods in Gladsheim, his great council hall, and asked Baldur to tell them what was troubling him.

'My father,' answered Baldur, 'of late terrible dreams have come to disturb my sleep—dreams threatening me with death and warning me of my great peril; dreams showing me the dark sad halls of Helheim and myself grown grey and corpse-like dwelling there with Nanna my beloved wife, from whom I can see the light of life faded even as from me.'

Odin was much troubled to hear this, for although he could not see into the future he knew that Baldur must die one day and that his death would be the first dark shadow of Ragnarok, the Twilight of the Gods.

So leaving Baldur and his brethren still talking in Gladsheim with Queen Frigga their mother, Odin saddled his eight-legged horse Sleipnir and set out at full speed over Bifrost Bridge. Across Midgard he went, riding in a storm cloud with his Valkyrie daughters to guard him; but he left them when he turned down the dark road leading to Helheim, the land of the dead, beneath the earth.

At last he came to the edge of Hela's land, and there the great Hell-hound Garm met him—Garm of the bloody breast—and barred his way, barking furiously.

Odin did not enter Helheim but rode round its mighty walls until he came to the grave of Volva the witch. Here he dismounted, drew the magic runes on the hard ground, and chanted a spell.

Slowly the ground gaped, and out of it rose the dead green shape of the witch, crying in ghastly tones:

'Who is this who adds torments to those I already endure?
I was buried in snow, I was washed by the icy rain, I was frozen
in the white rime, I have long been dead.'

'Tell news of Helheim!' cried Odin. 'Speak of the future.
Are the benches set in Hela's halls for any of my kin?'

'For Baldur the beautiful the mead is brewed,' she answered.
'Hodur's hand shall slay him and despair come to the gods. I have
spoken against my will: now let me depart. Trouble me not again
till the day of the battle, when Loki, yet unbound, shall break
his chains, and the wolf Fenris run free and the gods perish!'

Odin lowered his hand, and the witch sank once more into her
grave over which the earth closed. Then he leapt upon Sleipnir
and rode back to Asgard, full of sorrow, and wondering if by any
means the day of Baldur's doom might be delayed.

When he reached Asgard he heard shouts of joy and laughter.
The gods were playing once more on Idavollr as if all care had
left them.

'What has chanced that the great fear is no more?' asked Odin.

'I have saved Baldur,' answered Frigga joyfully. 'Now there is
no longer any danger, for nothing can harm him.'

'How has this come about?' asked Odin doubtfully, remembering the words of Volva the witch.

'All things in the world love Baldur and have sworn not to
harm him,' said Frigga. 'I have taken an oath from fire and water,
from iron and all other metals, from every stone and the earth
itself, from all diseases and poisons, from every beast and bird,
fish and creeping thing; nothing created will bring ill to Baldur.'

Comforted by this, Odin went to his throne from which he
looked out over the world, and Frigga returned to her mansion
called Fensalir, where she sat spinning the clouds.

Out on the plain of Idavollr the young gods had discovered a
new pastime. Baldur stood there laughing, his face shining with
joy, while one and another cast their spears at him, smote him
with swords, hewed at him with axes, pelted him with stones. For
the spears would not touch him, the swords made no mark, the
axes turned aside and the stones fell harmlessly to the ground.

The gods rejoiced that nothing would hurt their beloved Baldur, and held it an honour such as had been granted to no others and which none could ever deserve save only Baldur. All things rejoiced save one alone—and that was Loki. All the evil in him welled up into a cruel jealousy. If he could harm Baldur it would hurt the gods of Asgard more than anything else even he could imagine; and now he hated them above all things, and of them all he most hated shining Baldur, the world's darling.

So Loki stole away from Idavollr and took on the shape of an old, wise woman. Thus disguised he went to Fensalir, where Frigga sat spinning the clouds, and greeted her.

'There is a merry noise ringing across Asgard from Idavollr,' said Frigga, with her gentle smile. 'Can you tell me what my sons are doing?'

'That I can,' said the pretended old woman eagerly. 'They are all throwing darts and stones at Baldur and striking him with their weapons. Yet none of them hurts him at all.'

'True,' smiled Frigga. 'Neither metal nor wood nor stone can harm Baldur, for I have taken an oath from all things.'

'What, has every single thing in the whole world sworn not to hurt Baldur?' asked the disguised Loki.

'Yes, everything,' nodded Frigga happily. 'Oh, well, I did not trouble to ask an oath from the little soft mistletoe plant that grows on the oak tree to the east of Valhalla. For it seemed too young and feeble, and has not even got a root of its own but is forced to hang on the oak for support.'

Presently, having learned what he wanted to know, Loki slipped away, assumed his own form again, and hastened to the oak tree on the east of Valhalla. Here he found the mistletoe growing, and from it cut off a large sprig which he shaped into a dart.

Then he went back to the field of Idavollr, where Baldur was still serving as target for all who cared to cast at him. Only Hodur stood alone and dejected, taking no part in the sport.

'Why do you not also throw something at Baldur?' asked Loki.

'You know that I am blind,' answered Hodur bitterly. 'I cannot even see where Baldur is, and I have nothing to throw.'

'Come now,' said Loki, taking Hodur by the hand, 'do like the rest and show honour to Baldur by casting this twig at him; I will direct your aim so that you may be sure to strike him.'

Hodur took the mistletoe and let Loki guide his arm. Before it flew, Loki breathed on the soft stalk so that it grew hard and keen as steel. Then Hodur cast it, and it pierced Baldur through

the heart so that he sank lifeless to the ground. And never among gods or men was a worse deed done than this.

When Baldur fell, the gods were struck speechless with horror and grief and amazement, and Loki had slipped away before they thought to stop him. As for poor Hodur, though he had never meant to hurt Baldur, the eternal law decreed that he must die. Yet none might slay him in Asgard, and none of those who stood around slain Baldur had any mind to do so. So Hodur wandered away to dwell in the forests of night until the coming of Vali the avenger, Odin's youngest son, who was fated to be born to bring vengeance on him for the death of Baldur the beautiful.

Now the elder Aesir came hastening to Idavollr to join the younger gods, who still stood speechless about Baldur; and Odin bowed his head and wept at the loss of his beloved son and at the doom which now drew so near to Asgard and to Midgard too.

But Frigga cried: 'Who among you all will gain my love and goodwill for ever? Who will ride to Helheim and seek for Baldur, and offer Hela a ransom if only she will let him return to Asgard?'

Hermodur the swift-footed sprang forward: 'That will I!' he cried.

'Then take Sleipnir, my eight-legged horse,' said Odin, 'and get you to Helheim with all the haste you may. For there is no ransom too great that Hela can ask if only we may win back Baldur to the light of day.'

So Hermodur buckled on his shining armour, leapt upon Sleipnir, and was gone on his errand like a flash.

But the Aesir took the dead body of Baldur and bore it down over Bifrost and to the shore of the sounding sea. There stood Baldur's ship waiting—Hringhorn, the greatest of all ships and the fairest. On it they piled a great funeral pyre and set Baldur's body in the midst. The ship was now too heavy even for Thor to launch it, so they sent to Jotunheim for a friendly Giantess called Hyrrokin, who arrived riding on a huge wolf with snakes as her bridle. It took four of the strongest of the Einheriar to hold her steed while she set her shoulder to the ship and pushed so strongly that the rollers on which it ran down into the sea caught fire, and the whole earth shook.

Then each in turn bade farewell to Baldur. But when Nanna his wife bent over his body, her heart broke with grief, and they laid her beside him. All the gods gathered to do honour to Baldur, and even many of the Frost Giants and the Mountain Giants came to mourn at his funeral.

Last of all Odin bent over his dead son, setting the magic ring Draupnir on his finger, and whispering in his ear a Word which the fates put into his mind to speak, of which as yet even he did not know the meaning.

Then they set fire to the ship and cast her loose. The wind

caught the sails and carried her away across the waves; and as darkness fell there was a great burning far out at sea.

Meanwhile Hermodur was hastening on his journey to Helheim. For nine nights and nine days he rode through dark caves and deep glens and saw nothing till he came to Gioll, the river of fire which surrounded Helheim. Over it arched a bridge that shone like glittering gold, and on it stood the Death Maiden, Modgudur, guarding the way with her terrible skeleton hands.

'Who rides this way?' she cried. 'Even now five companies of the dead have crossed my bridge. But as for you, the hue of death is not upon you: why do you ride towards Helheim?'

'I am Hermodur, the son of Odin,' he answered, 'and I ride to Helheim in search of Baldur the beautiful. Have you seen him pass this way?'

'Baldur has already ridden over Gioll's bridge, and Nanna with him,' answered Modgudur. 'But you cannot pass this way. To the northward lies your road, until you come to Hela's gates.'

On went Hermodur until he came to the barred gates of Helheim where Garm stood on guard in the Gnipa Cave, barking savagely. There was no chance of passing through the gates, so Hermodur dismounted to tighten his girths, and then set Sleipnir at them at such a gallop that the great horse of Odin cleared the gates at a bound and landed safely in Helheim.

On rode Hermodur, and came to the great Halls of Hela. There he found his dead brother Baldur sitting with Nanna in the place of honour; and he passed the night in their company and among those of human race who do not fall in battle and so cannot come to Valhalla and join the Einheriar.

The next day he went and knelt before Hela, begging her to let Baldur ride back to Asgard with him.

'Baldur shall go free and return from among the dead on one condition,' said Hela. 'If, as you say, all living things love Baldur, let them all weep for him. And if everyone does, without a single exception, their tears shall weep Baldur out of Helheim, and back to the light of day. But if any refuses to weep, or speaks against

Baldur, here he shall remain and his light shall never again shine on the earth.'

Full of hope, Hermodur rode back by the long dark way towards Midgard, and so over Bifrost Bridge to Asgard, bearing with him the ring Draupnir as a token from Baldur to Odin.

When they heard Hela's terms, the gods sent messengers throughout all the world begging everything to weep so that Baldur might be delivered from Helheim. All wept. Even the Giants wept for Baldur the shining one, and every living creature. The very stones wept, as they still do if they pass suddenly from a cold place into a hot one.

It seemed that Baldur was saved. But as the messengers were returning, full of joy, towards Asgard they found an old Giantess sitting in a cavern and laughing. They begged her to weep Baldur out of Helheim, but with no success.

'I am Thaukt the old!' she screeched. 'And I will weep dry tears for Baldur. What has he done for *me*? Why should *I* weep for him? Let Hela keep what is hers.'

In vain the messengers argued with Thaukt: not a tear would she shed for Baldur. At last they returned, sad at heart, to Asgard and reported their failure to the Aesir.

Odin sat silent for a while. Then he said:

'It seems to me that the Giantess Thaukt was none other than Loki, who was our brother but is now our deadliest enemy. The time has come to take him and bind him in chains like his son Fenris the wolf, so that he can do no further evil until the day of Ragnarok, when all chains shall be broken.'

So now the hunt was up, and the gods scoured land and sea in search of him. Loki built himself a house with four doors high up in the mountains on the river bank beside a great waterfall.

'I'm safe here!' thought Loki. 'If the Aesir come, I shall be able to see them while they're far away, and I'll turn myself into a salmon and hide under the waterfall. They wouldn't know where I was, and couldn't catch me. . . . Suppose I was trying to catch a salmon who had hidden behind a waterfall, how would I do it? I'm much cleverer than any of them, so I ought to be able to think of a way. . . . Yes, I'd make a net such as Rann, Aegir's wife, uses to catch sailors when great storms wreck the ships of the men of Midgard. Only mine would be a smaller net, and I'd make it out of flax and yarn—something like this.'

He began weaving a mesh as he sat by the fire looking out on all sides. Suddenly he saw a party of the Aesir coming in the distance. With a curse he flung the partly made net into the fire and sprang into the river.

Presently Odin, Thor and Kvasir the wise reached Loki's house, and began looking about them. There was no sign of Loki, but Kvasir noticed the burnt outline of the net among the ashes of the fire.

'See what he was making,' he said; 'a net, such as Rann uses, but made of flax and yarn. . . . Such a net would catch fish, and I will teach the making and use of it to the men of Midgard. . . . But let us make one now and see what yonder pool beneath the waterfall contains. It comes into my mind that Loki has taken on the shape of a fish, and was trying to see if any means might be found to catch a water-dweller who would obviously not take a bait and swallow a hook.'

Swiftly clever Kvasir wove a great net, and the three gods dragged the pool with it until Loki was cornered. In a final desperate effort to escape the giant salmon leapt over the net. But Thor caught him by the tail and held him so firmly that salmon have narrow tails to this day.

When Loki at last returned to his own shape, the gods bound him with fetters of iron upon three sharp rocks in a great cavern under the earth, and left him. But the cruel Giantess Skadi, who hated him, hung a serpent over his head to drop burning poison on Loki's face.

Even Loki had at least one living creature to love him; for his wife Sigyn hastened to his side and stood there holding a cup to catch the drops of venom. When the cup was full and she turned aside to empty it, Loki roared and writhed in his bonds: the earth shook, and men said that there was an earthquake.

And there Loki was fated to remain until the day of Ragnarok.

RAGNAROK

AGNAROK, the Twilight of the Gods, was still to come and
the day of the Last Great Battle had not dawned—for it
would be the end of the world. But prophets in visions of
the future could see what was to come: the great seer Volo
revealed it all to Odin, and Harr the Heaven-inspired to Gylfi, the
king of Sweden, in the days before the beginning of history.

When Ragnarok draws near will come the Fimbul-winter;
during it, snow will fall from the four corners of the world, the
frosts will be severe and unceasing, the wind piercing, the weather

tempestuous, and the sun will give no heat. Three years will pass like this, making one long winter with never a gleam of summer. Then three more such winters will follow during which war and discord will spread over the whole earth : brother shall rise against brother and kill merely for gain, nor shall any man spare either his parents or his children. Hard will be that age, and evil shall prevail —'an axe-age, a sword-age, a storm-age, a wolf-age, ere doom comes upon the earth'.

After that the wolf who has for ever pursued the Sun across the sky shall catch and devour her; and the wolf who pursues the Moon shall catch and devour him also. Then the stars shall fall from Heaven, the mountains will come crashing together, the forests shall be torn from their roots, the earth shaken to pieces, and they that there were bound shall be loosened, and all fetters shall fall in pieces.

The wolf Fenris shall break the chain Gleipnir, and the Midgard serpent shall come up out of the sea on to the land. But when he does, Midgard will sink under the waters, and there shall be no more earth.

Fenris shall then advance against Asgard, his open jaws reaching from the sea to the sky, and beside him his brother Jormungand, the Midgard serpent, pouring forth floods of venom to overwhelm the air and the waters. As they come, the sky will split open and through the breach will ride Surtur with his fiery sword and the sons of Muspell, leaving all in flames behind them.

As the invaders pour over Bifrost Bridge it breaks to pieces behind them, and they gather for the Last Great Battle on the Plain of Vigrid, which is a hundred miles each way. There Fenris and Jormungand, with their father Loki and their sister Hela, draw up their line of battle, the whole host of the Giants following them.

Meanwhile Heimdall stands in the gateway of Asgard and blows the Giallar-horn to arouse the gods, who assemble outside Valhalla and march against the foe with all the Einheriar, the heroes, following them.

Odin leads the battle on Vigrid Field, his golden helmet shining and the spear Gungnir flashing in his hand, and attacks Fenris. By his side marches Thor, whirling his hammer Miolnir; but he can give Odin no help, for all his might is needed to stand against Jormungand the serpent.

The first to fall is brave Frey of the Vanir, fighting against fiery Surtur; and he would not have fallen had he not parted with his sword to his servant Skirnir, who won for him his bride the Giant maiden Gerdhr. That day also Garm the great hound of Helheim breaks loose from the Gnipa Cave and comes against Tyr; he is the most fearful monster of all, yet Tyr slays him and himself is slain.

Then Thor does the greatest deed of all, slaying Jormungand the Midgard serpent and crushing his head with Miolnir. As the serpent dies, Thor reels back nine paces and himself falls dead, drowned in the flood of venom that pours from slain Jormungand.

Now the wolf Fenris swallows Odin. But Odin's son Vidar the silent leaps upon Fenris, sets his foot upon the wolf's lower jaw, seizes his upper jaw and tears him asunder until he dies.

Heimdall attacks Loki, and the two fight desperately against each other, and each kills his adversary.

After this Surtur spreads flame and fire over all the world, and it is consumed.

Yet soon, out of the sea, rises another and a fairer world, green and lovely, where the corn grows in the fields without needing to be sown. Of Asgard itself the fair plain of Idavollr alone remains unharmed, and there dwell Vidar and Vali, who were not slain at Ragnarok. Thither also come Modi and Magni, the sons of Thor, bearing with them Miolnir, their father's hammer; and from dark Helheim returns Baldur the beautiful with Nanna his wife, and his beloved brother Hodur, who now can see.

There in the new Heaven sit the younger gods talking of the great battle, and remembering how Fenris and the Midgard serpent met their end, and how Loki died.

In the new earth lie hidden two who escaped both Surtur's fire

and the great flood: a woman called Lif and her husband Lif-
thrasir; she is Life, and he the Desire of Living. They feed on the
morning dew, and their descendants shall people the whole earth.
And there are bright halls in Heaven to which they shall come
when they die; and there dwell the souls of just men and women
even from the old world of Midgard that was destroyed.

Moreover, ere she perished, the Sun became the mother of a
daughter to rise and shine in the new sky above the new earth;
and she shall never perish. Nor shall the young gods, the children
of the Aesir, perish either; but One shall rise to rule both Earth
and Heaven, and to bring redemption to all the races of mankind.
For this is the Word which God put into Odin's heart to whisper
in the ear of his dead son Baldur—though as yet, in the world of
the old gods, he did not know its meaning.